Career Success in Healthcare Information Technology

Betsy S. Hersher, FHIMSS
Linda B. Hodges

HIMSS Mission
To lead change in the healthcare information and management systems field through knowledge sharing, advocacy, collaboration, innovation, and community affiliations.

Printed in the U.S.A. 5 4 3 2 1

Requests for permission to make copies of any part of this work should be sent to:

Permissions Editor
HIMSS
230 E. Ohio, Suite 500
Chicago, IL 60611-3269
nvitucci@himss.org

ISBN 0-9725371-5-5

For more information about HIMSS, please visit *www.himss.org*

Table of Contents

ABOUT THE AUTHORS

Betsy S. Hersher, FHIMSS, is the president and founder of Hersher Associates, Ltd., a nationally recognized leader in retained executive searching and consulting for all aspects of healthcare. From their corporate offices in Northbrook, Illinois, Hersher Associates, Ltd., recruits for a broad array of senior level healthcare positions for diverse clients in areas of IT, outsourcing, finance, security, patient care services, clinical redesign, managed care, physician practice management, health information management, marketing and human resources. Clients include integrated delivery networks, academic medical centers, healthcare technology vendors and consulting firms.

Hersher is a nationally acclaimed speaker, author and expert on career plan development, organizational design, physician recruitment in IT and position design consulting in healthcare. She is a strong proponent of successor roles to the CIO and is instrumental in developing and promoting roles such as the chief technology officer and chief medical information officer. In addition, Hersher is an assistant professor at the University of Illinois at Chicago.

Prior to founding Hersher Associates, Hersher led the executive search and project management at a leading healthcare market research and consulting firm. She was also a recreational therapist and coordinator of children's activities at an academic medical center.

Hersher served as vice president of administration for the Center for Healthcare Information Management (CHIM). She is an active Foundation member of the College of Healthcare Information Management Executives (CHIME) and is a Fellow of the Healthcare Information and Management Systems Society (HIMSS), which awarded her its 2003 Leadership Award. She is also a member of the American College of Healthcare Executives (ACHE), the Healthcare Financial Management Association (HFMA) and a charter member of the Association of Medical Directors of Information Systems (AMDIS).

Linda B. Hodges is the executive vice president of Hersher Associates and has been with the company since 1989. She manages the Hersher consulting staff, is responsible for business development and is the account manager for major clients at Hersher Associates.

Hodges has managed senior IT recruitment at many of the country's leading healthcare organizations. Prior to joining Hersher Associates, Hodges held various management positions with a national healthcare IT consulting and research firm. Her expertise is in the areas of executive recruitment, organizational assessment, position design and industry research.

Hodges speaks and writes on a variety of healthcare, career development and recruitment and retention related topics, including new roles and positions, trends in the industry and successful interviewing. She and Hersher co-author a monthly column in *ADVANCE for Health Information Executives* titled Career Counsel.

Hodges is a senior member of HIMSS, a member of HFMA and an active Foundation member of CHIME.

ACKNOWLEDGMENTS

Our thanks to Bonnie Siegel, Bridget Stern, Maggie Meier, Judi Infusino, and Graeme Udd, our editors and researchers, and to HIMSS, our partners on this project.

A special thanks to Nancy Vitucci, HIMSS senior editor, who has been wonderful throughout this process.

We would also like to thank HIMSS for working in collaboration with Hersher Associates, Ltd., on the HIMSS / Hersher 2002 Job Satisfaction Survey. Figures from the survey appear in this book.

In addition, we thank Frank Irving, *Advance for Health Information Executives* magazine, as well as Merion Publications. Excerpts in this book have appeared in issues of *Advance for Health Information Executives.*

Perspectives on Careers

A Foreword for Career Success in
Healthcare Information Technology

Healthcare IT is a rewarding, exciting and prospering field. There are a wide range of careers in the field and, as healthcare IT investments continue to increase, the career opportunities should expand.

Career Success in Healthcare Information Technology, by Betsy Hersher and Linda Hodges, does a superb job of helping the healthcare IT professional assess their career goals and manage their career plans.

I have been a CIO for sixteen years and have had the extraordinary pleasure of working with hundreds of talented, committed healthcare IT professionals. I have had career discussions with many of these folks. From these discussions, and observations on their career paths, I offer three suggestions to the reader of this book. These suggestions should complement the insightful and actionable advice in this book.

Follow your passions. Some people view careers as a path to make more money and some people view careers as a way to increase prestige and power. While money does matter and prestige and power can be very satisfying, most people want careers that are rewarding, challenging and enjoyable.

They want to be excited about their work. They want to like and respect their colleagues. And they want to be proud of the organizations that they serve. When they tell others what they do, and whom they work for, they want to feel a passion.

As you contemplate your career or consider joining another organization, make sure that your choices are primarily guided by passion. You become excited when you contemplate the new job. You are enthusiastic when you think about the next step.

Do not take a new job simply because it is "good for your career." There is little that is more miserable than knowing that you have to get up every morning to do a job that you don't like or work for an organization that you don't respect.

Listen to your heart.

Careers are an important part of life but they should not define your life. More important than career goals are life goals. At the end of your life, what do want to be able to say? If you were to judge your life to be a good one, what will you be able to say that you have done or what will have happened?

At the end of my life, I want to be able to say:

- That I was as madly in love with my wife then as I am today.
- That my three daughters have had lives as blessed as mine.
- That I will have been spared great hunger, deep and enduring physical pain, crushing hatred or excruciating pain. If I was not spared this, I hope that I exhibited courage.
- That those people with whom I worked say that I inspired them, taught them and led them well.
- That the healthcare industry in which I work, and the organizations that I work for, have been changed, become more effective, and have advanced because of the legacy that I have left.

Your version of these goals should serve as the guide for all of your major life decisions including your career decisions.

Career decisions can have a major impact on other aspects of your life and vice versa. Career decisions should always be made in a way that considers and supports the overall set of goals that you have.

Careers are often defined by a small number of "out of the blue" opportunities. There is great value to planning your career and executing that plan. If your career goals point out the need to develop new skills, then you should pursue acquiring those skills. If your career plans mean that you may have to relocate several times, then you should make sure that your family is comfortable with the periodic move to a new community.

And yet, for most people, major advances in their careers occur as a result of what appear to be "out of the blue" opportunities. A phone call from a recruiter might arrive tomorrow or a year from now. The departure of your predecessor in the IT organization might occur next month or never. A talk you listen to at the HIMSS Annual Conference might inspire you to pursue an area that you had never considered.

Career changing moments are often impossible to predict and impossible to plan. These moments come "out of the blue."

Nonetheless, you can prepare yourself for these moments. You can increase your responsibilities and extend your accomplishments, such that when your predecessor leaves, your reputation has been established. You can become engaged in healthcare IT associations or write articles for the trade press, such that your name winds up in the recruiter's Rolodex. You can know yourself and understand your passions, such that you are sure that the excitement generated by someone's speech is a true excitement.

Career planning creates conditions that lead to opportunities. You can create your own luck.

You should enjoy this book and find its guidance invaluable. And if you follow the sage advice of the book, and heed to the three observations above, you should do well in your career.

I look forward to the opportunity to work with you someday.

John P. Glaser, PhD, FHIMSS
Vice President and Chief Information Officer
Partners HealthCare System, Inc., Boston, MA

xii

Introduction

The purpose of this book is not about the "how to" of careers in healthcare information technology, but rather it's about the "what is." As technology becomes the vital link in supporting new healthcare initiatives, what is required for healthcare IT leaders to take full advantage of this rapid evolution in the healthcare industry?

The job market in healthcare is currently expanding, offering a wide range of opportunities for enterprising and prepared career-oriented candidates. Achieving success in healthcare information systems—or healthcare IT—as in most professions, can be defined by your ability to take advantage of opportunities that will allow you to manage your own career growth. Today, professionals pursue opportunities for various reasons, not just monetary. With all things being equal, healthcare IT professionals pursue opportunities for growth, challenge and a positive corporate culture.

We are all motivated differently. Success is defined by our own indicators. The key to reaching your unique goals is to be self-aware, proactive and flexible. Indicators of success are no longer judged by the size of your IT budget and staff complement. Actually, the newest roles in healthcare IT require working in partnership and collaboration to influence change and foster progress. The ability to manage change and relationships will be a major factor defining your success.

It is critical to discover how your organization will evaluate your success and define your accomplishments. Understanding the methodology of evaluating success will keep you on top of your game.

IT is changing so rapidly that flexibility and creativity can help you balance your need for growth with essential projects that require your current expertise, while ensuring you are accomplishing what your manager expects from you—producing results. Healthcare organizations today are much more focused on accountability and a growing reliance on technology to support future healthcare initiatives.

No one can manage and develop your career better than you. As you work on identifying what success means to you, it is the perfect time to assess your strengths, weaknesses and future aspirations, for you will need that knowledge as you choose a new organization or change levels within your current culture.

The healthcare industry is constantly evolving. As a result, now is an excellent time for IT professionals to step up, be noticed, get ahead, assume new roles and gain additional experience. The job market in healthcare IT is wide open due to significant outside influences, including significant demands from government (i.e., HIPAA), business coalitions (i.e., LeapFrog), the Joint Commission on the Accreditation of Healthcare Organizations (JCAHO), and the general population.

The outside influences coupled with new key research and development will be forcing us to have IT available and at the center of most major and minor decisions. As a matter of fact, there will be a tacit assumption that the data is clean, up-to-date, easy to manipulate and that the knowledge gained from the data will be handled in a private and secure manner.

These are exciting, albeit challenging, times for IT professionals in the healthcare industry. IT professionals are finding innumerable options and career paths from which to choose. Often the choices are overwhelming and confusing, but by identifying long-term goals and creating a solid career plan, well-prepared individuals can make the right career decisions and enjoy fulfilling and rewarding careers. Based on over 25 years of experience as executive recruiters and consultants for the healthcare IT industry, we will share career development advice aimed specifically at future careers in healthcare IT.

CHAPTER 1

State of the Healthcare Industry: How It Affects Your Career

With so many new developments in all areas of healthcare, job opportunities in healthcare IT are there for the picking. After Y2K, chief executive officers (CEOs) became reluctant to provide additional money to IT and instead gave the resources to other areas of their enterprises. However, the tide has turned, and multiple influences are causing a shift in cash allocation.

The year 2003 was one of the most mercurial years in our economy, and 2004 continued the trend, with little relief in sight. Clearly, healthcare organizations are feeling the same pinch as those in other industries. They need to fill important positions and put new systems in place, but they have to work within the constraints of reduced capital and operational dollars. Nonetheless, we're not necessarily looking at a picture of gloom and doom. In fact, healthcare, even with cost constraints, remains one of the industries that continues to hire, and IT is getting approval for key positions.

The most important reason for continued hiring will affect the IT job market for years to come. Healthcare is changing drastically, with the industry seeking solutions for expanding many programs—ambulatory services, computerized provider order entry (CPOE), security / privacy and clinical redesign. In all new healthcare initiatives, IT is an integral part of the equation.

This isn't a time to rest on your laurels. It is a perfect time for you to review your resume and career track plan and to work toward becoming a valued and essential team player who can help your organization get through these times of change. Your efforts will help relieve the many pressures your organization is facing, both from the government and from the business community.

As baby boomers—the largest percentage of the population—age, their healthcare needs become a bigger and bigger issue. Systems for providing such care will be implemented through connectivity to physician offices and hospitals. Given all the potential initiatives, great opportunities for expansion in healthcare IT will arise.

In addition, most chief information officers (CIOs) are adding new positions to their staffs: one or more individuals who can be strong leaders assisting the CIOs and a chief medical information officer (CMIO). Many established CIOs and even some of their second-level managers are beginning to think about retirement. That means that some key leaders may soon retire, opening the door for a new era. Only recently has healthcare IT leadership started training successors. CIOs are looking to the market to give them the opportunity to do other things, such as work for a vendor, consult, become an interim CIO or start their own businesses.

Many organizations are mounting huge clinical systems initiatives and demanding that their CIOs have clinical backgrounds or systems experience. In such cases, the reporting relationship frequently changes so that the CIO reports to the CEO.

Shortly after the Y2K effort, we noted a growing concern that CIOs needed to be more technical and less strategic; therefore, we began to see a resurgence of CIOs reporting to chief financial officers (CFOs). That trend was very brief and was quickly replaced by a return to the extremely strategic CIO and a resurgence of hiring for the position of chief technology officer (CTO). Due to the creation of this position, many new roles can be less technically oriented and more business and application skills oriented.

The major clinical systems initiatives in progress have created a huge demand for CMIOs to play an active role in these implementations. Nurses and other clinicians with IT experience are also key to these initiatives. During the design and implementation of clinical systems, it is easier to utilize clinicians because of their unique perspective on patient care and ability to communicate efficiently with other clinicians. However, due to the complexity of some clinical IT implementations, we see nonclinical project managers in charge if they have previous relatable experience. Expertise in project management and successful clinical systems implementation can sometimes be more important than hands-on clinical expertise.

One of the key reasons that IT has a renewed strategic position is that many mission-critical issues have joint strategic and IT components, including e-commerce, e-health, the Health Insurance Portability and Accountability Act of 1996 (HIPAA), CPOE, security / privacy, clinical redesign and continuum of care. Here is a key benchmark: the world of the healthcare CIO is slightly over 20 years old and has finally become a key strategic force on the management team. Not too surprisingly, there are many new positions to fill in IT, which opens up huge opportunities for qualified candidates.

CHAPTER 2

Career Development in Healthcare IT

Career development and growth in the healthcare IT marketplace has been very unique and swift. Our industry, relatively speaking, is quite young. The field started developing in the late 1970s with a few slowdowns and bumps in the road. Despite the government's lack of understanding and funding for healthcare IT, the industry has moved steadily forward.

In less than 30 years, we have moved IT up the corporate structure and developed phenomenal new positions. As a result, we are as strategically focused as our neighbors in other industries. We are also extremely well positioned to utilize the technology that has been put in front of us. Our initiatives, resources, talent and technology are poised to set in motion the second generation of IT executives.

THE UNIQUENESS OF WORKING IN HEALTHCARE IT

The mission of healthcare itself clearly makes the industry unique. We take care of people and communities. We don't "build red trucks." For many, the mission of healthcare is the driver, i.e. the patient, and that makes it a more satisfying vocation. In addition to the healthcare mission, in general, there are many faith-based organizations and healthcare organizations that make some careers even more meaningful.

Probably the most important unique factor in terms of job progression is the expanding nature of our growth. We have moved rapidly, although many would say not rapidly enough. We've moved into critical, strategic roles affecting care delivery across the healthcare enterprise. These roles have grown and developed so quickly that sometimes the need for a specific skill comes and goes so rapidly, we hardly know where it has gone; e-health would be a fine example. It became an imperative in the e-health role for an IT candidate to have an e-health background, which was hard to find because there were very few experienced e-health IT folks. The various roles that have developed are often mission critical and require excellent communication and marketing skills, as well as technical skills to ensure that the different levels and factions within our organizations are clear and comfortable with new IT initiatives.

Another factor that makes us uniquely different is our structure and the varying levels, divisions and departments that need to be served. Is working with the chief of staff different than working with the general manager of a plant? YES! Is dealing with the head of internal medicine different than dealing with the head of the supply chain? YES! Healthcare has evolved so rapidly that we can barely keep up. The complexity of the environment is unique. As all the resources come together and start marching down the road to growth, what does that mean to your career?

Executive roles in IT are now broader. They aren't as technology-based as previously needed because we have filled many of the technical roles with individuals who are uniquely qualified to support the direction of healthcare IT with their technological knowledge and expertise. Our CIOs have moved rapidly into providing strategic support and proactively in seeking ways in which the technology supports the organization's overall initiatives and care delivery.

The flexibility required by all members of a healthcare IT organization is phenomenal, and part of that phenomenon is what makes career planning very different and rewarding. You can apply for a variety of different positions now and broaden your career path because of the plethora of healthcare needs that must be satisfied quickly, as healthcare marches forward. Computer services and health services continue to be in the top three fastest employment growth sectors in the country based on the Bureau of Labor statistics.

We aren't implying that a new graduate from a healthcare-oriented program can knock on the CIO's door and say, "Here I am, your new director of clinical systems." We aren't that flexible yet and probably never will be. However, many of the available positions require generalized executive traits and offer broader opportunities for career growth.

The supporting technology in a service-oriented organization will evolve as the mission of healthcare grows. Careers can grow quickly within healthcare IT. Many of the new roles being created are partly technical, but most require understanding that will support administrative and clinical redesign, EHR issues, HIPAA, security, inpatient, outpatient and home care uses of technology. This will affect healthcare in the next 10 years. Clinical candidates are in high demand in all areas of healthcare—including IT. An upwardly mobile candidate needs strong recognized leadership traits, including excellent communication at all levels, i.e., board collaboration, marketing ability to sell concepts, solid knowledge of the clinical enterprise, business savvy, customer service ability, and successful project management skills.

As an example, who would have thought 25 years ago as healthcare moved out of the basement into the mainstream and began dealing with clinicians that those very same clinicians might be taking lead roles in multi-million dollar IT implementations? Who would have thought that laboratory technicians, pharmacists, nurses and physicians would be joining the ranks of IT executives and leaving their white jackets behind. There is opportunity for trained healthcare professionals, as well as non-healthcare IT professionals, to make a significant impact and contribution to the industry.

THE EVOLUTION OF HEALTHCARE IT JOBS

As healthcare IT moves into its second generation of executive leadership, it is doing so with very different funding and technology. Since the new millennium, this has been an extremely unusual time for IT career growth. It seemed that as soon as we entered the 21st century, the door opened with an array of new leadership roles, as detailed in Chapter 17. Almost at the same time, some of our major healthcare institutions went deeper into financial crisis. Mergers, de-mergers and outsourcing caused significant angst for the healthcare IT world. These major issues affected individuals' career growth and ability to make a difference and the industry's ability to move forward.

Appropriately, in the last few years, some major positions have emerged that could be filled by candidates with healthcare or non-healthcare backgrounds. The influx of select non-healthcare leadership across the industry has been very valuable and has beefed up our knowledge-base in IT delivery. After a few years of apprenticeship in healthcare, these new leaders have joined the ranks of other well-regarded healthcare IT experts. As you develop your career path, visualize your career as a tree trunk with multiple branches. The trunk is comprised of skills that are required for professional growth, including education, implementation experience, leadership and management. These skills in various technology and healthcare arenas will allow you to follow any number of branches in your march toward leadership.

In the healthcare industry, your success isn't solely guaranteed by your good work. Your success is also dependent on your organization staying in business and valuing IT as a key corporate resource. Therefore, the skills you need to develop early on are listening and paying attention to the politics and financial issues surrounding you. The phrase "a degree in reading the tea leaves plays an important rung on your career ladder" may be said with a smile, but it holds some truth. Is your career growth in healthcare IT more secure if you have some specific healthcare background? Absolutely! There are so many new initiatives that you can practically pick and choose at will.

CHAPTER 3

Developing a Career Plan

You are the key to your own career growth. While you want security, you must take a risk. Although you have to be patient, you must also be tenacious.

The most effective way to reach your career goals is to develop a plan and be proactive, not reactive. Without a career plan to guide you, you may find yourself waiting around for the right opportunity instead of aggressively and intentionally pursuing your goals. You may stay in the wrong job too long or make decisions that are short-term fixes. Your plan should be designed to meet your needs and goals and keep you challenged. However, it should remain realistic and flexible, as determined by a changing healthcare market. You can ensure your plan stays current by continually reviewing and updating it.

WRITING, REVISING AND ACTIVATING A CAREER PLAN

How do you write a career plan? How do you know when to revise it? How do you know which portions to activate and when? Decide what your long-term career goals are. Think about where you want to be long-term. Research the technical and managerial skills needed to keep your career plan on the right path. There is rarely only one clear path. Remember to be realistic and flexible. Keep in mind the skill sets, duties and responsibilities required for your goals.

It is easy to fall into the trap of making the most logical career path your goal—however, this may not be right for you. For that reason, *it is recommended that you not put your career objective on your resume.* By providing such information, you may be boxing yourself in. Each of us will face multiple options in the course of our careers, and there may be several different routes to the same goal.

A career plan needs to be specific. You need to be prepared to reach your goals in every area that you wish to pursue, whether it be in education or in your ability to speak to large groups. For every benchmark in your career map, you must identify the skills, educational experience or management opportunities that will help you move forward and climb the next step.

Do degrees matter? Generally, yes they do, although what you received your degree in is of little relevance. Many individuals have entered healthcare IT after using computers in graduate school to work on their studies, research and theses. Many people who are strong leaders in healthcare IT switched from their initial area of study into computer science as a result of using computers in graduate programs.

Formal education is easy to deal with because it's fairly black and white. What's not easy is the informal education you need and how you acquire it within your organization. Do you have the coach to guide your learning process?

Because it is your personal strategic plan, it shouldn't depend on people, organizations and situations you can't control. Building your career plan on your current situation can be the biggest barrier to your success. For example, if you are working for a boss who doesn't value coaching, mentoring and developing your skills so that you can reach the next steps in your career plan, you will have a difficult time achieving your personal goals.

Your career plan should be updated at least once a year, at which time you should add the new skills that you've acquired, as well as any and all new accomplishments you've chalked up. Record everything you do and everything you learn in a "personal growth folder." You can then use that folder both to update your plan and to revise your resume.

Try to avoid making statements such as "Five years from now, I want to manage twenty-five people." In five years, if you're managing ten people and not twenty-five, you may feel discouraged. Instead, however, you should look at the responsibilities in your new role. Think of the big picture.

THE BEST WAYS TO MANAGE YOUR CAREER PLAN

Time Lines. You can use time lines to set marks telling you where you want to be at specific points in the future. You can tell yourself, for instance, "I want to earn my MBA by the time I am 40," or "I want to gain experience in contract negotiations or design for the new data center in the next year."

Position Titles. Position titles, per se, don't always indicate success or growth. Position content and sometimes reporting structure are more important than titles. Titles aren't uniform for all organizations so don't dwell on them. In academic organizations, the CEO is often called the executive director, and vice presidents are called directors. A title can be important; however, if it places you at the wrong organizational level to accomplish your job, that can be a problem. In such cases, be wary of promises to evaluate your title in six months and adjust it if necessary.

Realism. Be realistic in your plan and make sure that it is achievable based on your experience and ability to learn. Unachievable goals or unreasonable expectations will only leave you frustrated.

Working toward a realistic goal using an appropriate time line with benchmarks along the way is like following a recipe. Great cooks have the ability to adapt and substitute as they go along. But they also know that certain parts of a recipe must be done in order. In career planning as in cooking, skipping around can lead to undesired results. Know when and where to take shortcuts.

Figure 3-1 shows a road map to success. You will notice that this map is presented without a time line. Although we recommend following a path similar to the one in Figure 3-1, we emphasize that it is critical to be open to other opportunities.

You are probably wondering if you really have to write everything down. The answer is yes, because committing your plans to paper gives them greater credibility. Checking off the goals on your list as you accomplish them will also give you great satisfaction. We frequently become so involved in our day-to-day work that our successes and accomplishments begin to fade. Dates blur. Consequently, taking the time to regularly document dates and details of accomplishments is very important.

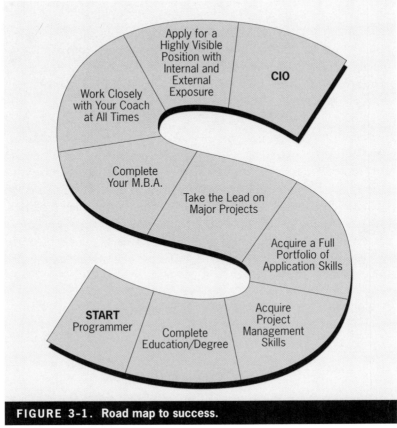

FIGURE 3-1. Road map to success.

Source: Hersher Associates, LTD. 2004.

PERSONAL FACTORS CAN AFFECT CAREER PLANS

While developing your career plan, remember to consider your family and their special interests, needs and goals. For example, if you really want a higher-level position but you live in a town that has only two healthcare organizations and no such positions are available, you may need to pursue opportunities in different parts of the state or the country. How would relocation affect your family? Can you uproot them?

Also look at personal commitments and other external factors that may affect your plan and time lines, such as having young children, elderly parents or educational demands. Does someone in your family have special needs? Aging parents or a child in high school may need extra consideration. Agreeing to commute for one or two years isn't always the answer. Be realistic. You may have to put relocation on the back burner for a few years. We are seeing a strong resurgence of candidates accepting or turning down job offers due to location and family priorities. Such factors may lead you to look at your current company as a long-term commitment and, in turn, to expect your employer to return that loyalty.

Look at different interim steps that make sense. You must remain focused on your ultimate goal, yet be adaptable. If your ultimate goal is to be a CIO, you may take the traditional route up through the ranks or you may decide to work for a consulting firm or a vendor to broaden your perspective. There is no right or wrong approach. Just remember that operational experience is preferred if your ultimate goal is a management position.

When you've completed the first draft of your career plan or map, sit down with your boss and discuss whether your plans are achievable and if your boss is able and willing to help you. Choose your words very carefully so that your boss understands that your plan is a path—not a demand—and you hope that he or she can coach you.

CHAPTER 4

How to Grow in Your Career

Developing a career road map doesn't mean you must leave your current job. It is your responsibility to create your own career growth path.

Even though you may have a focused plan, serendipity can present a great opportunity if it meets your criteria for growth. Why not? This is definitely a time to utilize your personal coaching team (see Chapter 6) to find things you may have overlooked. Always keep in mind that you are the final decision maker.

Remember, you aren't alone. There are many friends and professional resources that can help you grow. Identifying good coaches or mentors and developing productive relationships are critical to career development. Most people are willing to give advice and serve as coaches. Seek their counsel and constructive criticism. However, there is a fine line between accepting and rejecting criticism in a gracious manner.

IMPORTANT STEPS IN CAREER GROWTH INCLUDE

- Focus / plan
- Make a commitment
- Find good mentors
- Accept responsibility
- Develop the ability to deal with pressures and politics
- Sharpen your management and leadership skills

- Know what you need to learn
- Choose your venue carefully
  - Internal
  - External
- Volunteer for projects
- Keep an active list of awards and accomplishments
- Deliver on what you promise
- Become a member of an association

Depending on how high you raise the bar, you will most likely require some degree of training and education, mentoring, experience and time. You need to be realistic and patient—this will take time, commitment and dedication.

Building a relationship with recruiters is also helpful in career development. Good ones can give you advice on resume writing, alert you to existing opportunities, coach you on presentation and interview skills and help you prepare for specific interviews. Even though recruiters have specific positions to fill, it is important to build a good rapport. Explain to recruiters your background and interests. Let them know the kind of organization you would like to work for and discuss your relocation options. If a recruiter really gets to know you, you will be much more likely to get a call about the right job. Good recruiters can also help you decide if an opportunity is right for you.

Make short-term goals to obtain the skills you need, but keep the larger, long-term goal in mind at all times. Each step should get you closer to your ultimate career goal. Many things can, and probably will, happen to throw you a curve: mergers, financial problems, new bosses, changes in responsibilities and lifestyle or family issues, to mention a few. Try to remain flexible and use the changes to your advantage whenever possible. You never know when a great opportunity to advance will present itself, and it could be an opportunity that you never considered before. Some of the best job changes are serendipitous.

Until fairly recently, people who considered themselves "techies" could expect a career progression that pointed up a somewhat narrow technical ladder. On the other hand, people who considered themselves managers, even though they may have had some technical background, chose to go up a different career ladder.

The reality of healthcare today is that technology—anything involved with getting information from one place to another—has as much influence on an organization's bottom line as the applications it uses. Integration, communication and security technology will be among the clear drivers in the future.

The explosion of new technologies and much more complex healthcare IT initiatives are opening up many new senior-level positions. In the past, people who wanted to pursue senior-level positions felt that they needed to have very generalized and broad skills. They needed to know not only technology but also applications and management to aspire to be a director or a CIO, which were the only real senior IT positions in hospitals and health systems. However, such positions are becoming more and more executive in nature, and technical and management skills are required of most individuals.

In contrast, our experience indicates that many of today's professionals embrace technology, are genuinely excited by working with it and, thanks to new positions, are able to follow purely technical tracks and still advance to senior-level IT positions. If you are pursuing a senior technology track, you still need to be prepared to work in the executive suite. But fortunately, there are opportunities to advance along a career track without necessarily having to take the generalist approach previously required for senior-level positions. There are common requirements for continued career growth, including an understanding of general healthcare issues affecting your organization, project management, people management, leadership skills and the ability to communicate technical issues in an understandable manner.

At the same time, we're seeing excellent opportunities for people coming from other departments, who aren't necessarily technical, but who are more interested in applications and systems. People who fit this profile tend to pursue the CIO route—or at least they want to get to a director-level position in which they'll be involved with how applications and information are used. For these individuals to grow into CIO roles, they must acquire enough technical knowledge and exposure to be respected and to make credible decisions.

What if you are very technical but you have absolutely no interest in management? It is possible to pursue a career path that will lead to a well-paying, well-respected position without having to deal with budgets, personnel reviews and other administrative responsibilities. Such a position is often called the director of technology planning or architecture. This person concentrates on what's at the forefront of technology and ensures that the appropriate technical decisions are made. It is becoming a critical position due to the rapid rate of change in technology.

To advance to a senior-level IT position with responsibility for other people, projects and budgets, you must have proven management experience. And you must demonstrate the interpersonal skills and executive qualities that would be required of any other person at that level in the organization.

So, given the different career paths toward professional fulfillment, what are the best ways to grow in your career?

There are many variables attached to a career road map beyond the job itself. Your ideal job is the goal, but other factors, including your personal requirements, your preferred work environment, the required education and your willingness to relocate—to mention a few—are extremely important.

When devising your road map, be realistic but stretch a little. Take it step-by-step. Before you start your map, talk with people you trust and find out their thoughts on future possibilities. It would also be beneficial to seek the advice of people you respect or admire, people who have already taken your route and can give you some pointers.

THINGS TO CONSIDER WHEN PLANNING YOUR CAREER ROAD MAP

Concentrate on crossover. Often, people who choose a technical path enjoy working independently and focusing on their specific area of interest. If you fall in this category, be careful not to ignore everything else that is going on in your organization and be certain that you understand how your projects fit into the big picture.

Don't sell yourself short. Your general skills may be put to the test before you know it. Y2K and merger mania forced savvy CIOs to put people into certain positions based primarily on their project management skills. Your CIO may recognize your ability to handle projects and say, "We've got this huge application to implement. Can you handle the project?" Don't be afraid to tackle the challenge. A good CIO will get you the help you need to succeed on the technical side.

Get involved. Regardless of which career path you take, it's up to you to demonstrate what you're capable of accomplishing. Express your ideas in meetings. Volunteer for projects or implementations beyond your circle of familiarity. Ask if you can attend conferences and seminars.

Evaluate your strengths. If you are a programmer and you'd like to become a manager of programming, think about the skills and exposure you'll need to succeed the current manager in his or her position. Go to your manager and ask, "What do I need to do to succeed? How do you view me? What skills do I need to develop? Will you teach me?"

Use common sense. A key factor in keeping yourself on track toward your career goal is the ability to "say when." Recognize when you've done something to the best of your ability, and don't be afraid to ask for additional resources. Start thinking about what will make you more effective in your job right now, rather than automatically agreeing to more work without analyzing the situation. Being able to ask for help is an important first step toward becoming a leader.

As a reminder: your career development road map needs to be constantly reviewed and updated. Throughout your career, various paths can lead you in several different directions. When you come to that fork in the road, choose your route wisely. Take the time to reassure yourself that the decision you make is in alignment with your ultimate goals.

Being able to recognize opportunities and design your own career path is an art. Don't wait for things to come to you—be proactive. You must know what you are looking for and exhaust all avenues to get it.

Set goals and time lines. Make sure your goals are realistic. Give yourself ample time to develop and accomplish these goals. Look at where you are now with your skills and your position, then determine where you want to go. Take into consideration the corporate culture that you feel is most appropriate for you and that will allow you to thrive. Think about the kind of boss you want. Also, determine what kind of mission your desired organization will pursue.

CONSIDER YOUR ENVIRONMENT

Think about several jobs that would make you happy. For example, if you are in charge of applications at an academic medical center but your goal is to become a CIO, you might continue to be happy in an academic medical center or you might be equally challenged in a somewhat smaller integrated delivery system environment. Check your educational background. Most organizations insist on a bachelor's degree and many prefer a master's degree. The master's degree that would be most important would be an MBA. Clearly, if you have a concentration in marketing or in IT, that would be a plus.

It's very important to describe the environment where you feel you would be most productive. Do you like the philosophy of the management team? Do you like the mission of the IT organization? Most importantly, do you like your boss? Can you learn from him or her? And will you find yourself in a team that is supportive?

If you want to be a CIO, determine the skills that you will need. Clearly, professional leadership experience would be extremely important. The ability to communicate at all levels—writing, speaking and listening—is essential. Broaden your understanding of the organization's issues beyond IT. You should seek out a coach and mentor. Attend meetings that are very complex, meetings where you will have an opportunity to observe senior management. It would be valuable to work closely with the CIO to see if you could get into a position of higher visibility.

Consider networking at national meetings, talk to CIOs from other organizations and keep your ears open for CIO positions that you would be qualified for. Of course, it is highly recommended that you explore opportunities internally to see if there is a next level of growth available, such as an associate CIO position. In that kind of role, you would have an excellent opportunity to meet the senior management team and understand what it is like to work with them. Executive skills can be learned, as can leadership skills, but the desire must be there. Know what resources to tap for education and exposure. Encourage your boss to evaluate you often during this process so you will have an idea of what you still need to learn.

We used to tell up-and-coming managers that if they didn't awake in a cold sweat at four o'clock in the morning, wondering how their projects were going to be completed, they weren't ready to move up. Feel, breathe and live the responsibilities you will face as you progress through your career path. Check along the way that you are indeed on the right track and that you have completed each step appropriately.

CHANGING A CAREER PLAN

There are times when a change in one's career plan takes place. Many healthcare professionals view IT as the prime moving force in healthcare today. They are excited by the concept but may not be prepared for some of the realities. Senior executives in administration or finance, for example, decide to move into the IT arena after participating in the selection and implementation of new systems. Many physicians and nurses have also given up clinical medicine to take active roles in IT. Those transitions often are fairly seamless because the person has usually established a track record and trust within the organization.

Careful consideration should be given before initiating a change because that change will likely affect title, job level and compensation. Individuals who decide to move from other areas into technology should recognize the challenge and ensure that their commitment is solid enough to weather the change and its ramifications. They should seek counsel and advice from those who are close to them, both personally and professionally. Career change can be very rewarding, but scrutiny is important and should take place in advance of the change.

CHAPTER 5

Skills Assessment

The healthcare industry has a long history of hiring senior executives as if they were in a club. Some 30+ years ago the good old boy / girl culture was in place in healthcare. It seemed to help if you knew the right people and went to the right schools. Until recently, (in the last fifteen years or so) an MBA was looked down upon because, after all, healthcare wasn't a business. Membership in the club didn't automatically prepare senior executives to manage their healthcare organizations through mergers and the development of integrated delivery systems.

For many years, if strong business skills were put into a senior executive position description, there was a great human cry. Healthcare organizations managed to perceive government and insurance company reimbursement as a "blank check." When that stopped, because of the Tax Equity and Fiscal Responsibility Act of 1982 (TEFRA) executives began to realize how desperately they needed to hire candidates with an MBA and a track record of change management and turnarounds. Healthcare has evolved fairly rapidly from an antiquated industry into one that appreciates and requires business skills. The industry had to deal with managed care growth and then the evolution of integrated delivery networks, along with mergers, clinical redesign and now, an electronic health record utilizing CPOE. As you evaluate your skill list, it is important to note that the vast majority of these skills allow you to operate in this newfound environment.

Fitting into the corporate culture and seeking a good working environment are now more important than things that seemed to matter before. So if you are wondering how your skills would transfer into business, it could be stated that there has been a significant metamorphosis. As healthcare executives, leaders and managers are given the right opportunities to exercise these business skills, this will in no small measure help change the healthcare industry. In the last eight to nine years, when written position descriptions mentioned business skills, physicians yelled, "What do you mean business skills?" This concept has been a very long time coming, and we think it is here to stay. Bottom line: leadership skills coupled with a proven track record in IT will carry a great deal of weight in your career advancement.

GETTING STARTED

Because of the multitude of challenges facing healthcare IT professionals today, you need to be entirely honest with yourself when determining your career goals. Likewise, you need to be open and honest with yourself when you are evaluating your personal style, attributes, strengths, limitations and requirements to get ahead. In other words, what skills do you possess? What are your weaknesses? What do you need or want to learn? What do you enjoy doing? And what have you been doing for years (even though they may be well-recognized skills) that you want to leave behind?

In developing a career plan, do an honest, objective and thorough assessment of your skills and attributes. When listing your strengths, weaknesses and potentials, it is very important to focus on the here and now, not on where you want to be. Many of us have strengths of which we are totally unaware, and yet they are exactly the strengths that will help us grow in our environment or move on to another job. Did you ever think that a good sense of humor would be something a CEO would seek in a new hire? It's there in almost every position description.

Take a look at some of the crucial advancement skills we've outlined for you at the end of this chapter, as well as at some of the motivations to learn those skills. They seldom have anything to do with technical or straight application proficiency. Instead, they relate to partnering, being flexible, learning, demonstrating leadership, managing change and being a team player.

As you look at your list of strengths, weaknesses and potentials, which you have certainly reviewed with your close friends, peers, bosses or business advisers to make sure that you're on target, view the things you're calling weaknesses as growth areas. Not every weakness has to be considered a negative. For example, you may list your inability to understand finances as a deficit. Yet, there's a big difference between understanding finances and being able to do complicated spreadsheets. What you need to do is learn how to read spreadsheets and how to ensure that the people who design them use the correct data to produce the needed results.

As far as your weaknesses are concerned, work with your mentor or boss on how you can improve, but be careful not to bite off more than you can chew. Take one step at a time and make sure you have comprehensively examined the areas that need improvement. Define each area and map out specific actions so that improving becomes a project. Put together a plan with your mentor or boss to reach your goal.

In the section on potential, completing the sentence "I have the potential to be . . ." is critical. When you're looking for a new role, whether with your current employer or elsewhere, you want to be in an organization that will help you reach your potential by providing growth opportunities and mentoring.

FLEXIBILITY IS KEY

Just because you began your career as a technical expert, don't fall into the old myth that you must remain technical. If you aspire to attain a more general management position or to ultimately become a director or CIO, your career plan must include the steps to make that transition possible.

Rarely will you identify only one clear path to where you want to go, so be flexible and keep in mind the skill set you will need to match your goals. The truth is that you probably already possess a majority of the basic skills; they just need to be honed by experience, education and the proper mentoring. Experience and exposure allow most of us to grow. Additionally, it is critical to note that personal / soft skills and values are the ones, in the long run, that are the most important for growth, recognition and self-satisfaction. This is in contrast to hard skills which tend to have more business or analytical focus.

Conducting a realistic skills assessment requires courage, honesty, flexibility and a comfort level that allows you to be vulnerable. You are vulnerable because you need outside support and help to correctly do an assessment. You also need friends, mentors, bosses, coworkers and family members to help you verify or dispute what you have written—and it's a must to write down your assessment. Record your thoughts so that you can evaluate, add, delete and modify them. Often, if we don't write things down, we don't take them seriously.

There are many ways to view skills. We aren't all good at everything, nor should we be. Think about what you aren't good at doing, what you need to learn and where you need to grow, and then match them to a plan.

Once you have identified your strengths, you should move on to the areas you would like to improve, the areas you would like to learn and your areas of weakness. You might even employ an industrial psychologist to conduct a battery of tests to evaluate your strengths and weaknesses. Be prepared to be surprised.

To evaluate skills needed for future growth and advancement, you need to review where you have been, what you have learned, what projects you enjoy and what projects you never want to do again. Keep in mind your long-term goals and the short-term skills you need to get there.

You must be honest with yourself in your evaluation. Asking the opinion of someone you trust, who knows you well and who isn't afraid to be honest, can be very helpful and keep you on target. Skills fall into two categories that we like to refer to as "hard skills" and "soft skills." Both kinds are equally important in your evaluation. Hard skills are learned, innate or associated with experiences. Soft skills, in reality, are the ones that hiring executives seek. Review the lists that follow carefully. Your ability to fit into a corporate culture will be evaluated by the skills listed.

SKILLS THAT SENIOR EXECUTIVES SEEK

Hard Skills

- Leadership / management experience
- Business acumen
- Results / action oriented
- Team player
- Track record for delivering as promised
- Ability to partner
- Change agent
- Project management expertise
- Ability to retain excellent employees with growth potential
- Ability to market new ideas
- Ability to hire candidates capable of carrying out the strategic vision under your direction
- Negotiator
- Coalition builder
- Politically savvy
- Educator
- Ability to deal with changes
- Entrepreneur
- Strategic vision
- Technical knowledge

Soft Skills

- Image / presence / style
- Communication skills
- Listening skills
- Written communications
- Global view
- Vulnerability
- Decisiveness
- Self confidence
- Risk taker
- Maturity
- Comfort taking charge
- Comfort following
- Credibility as a leader
- Ability to manage relationship priorities
- Presentation and public-speaking skills
- Planning skills
- Sales skills
- Honesty
- Ability to be proactive
- Openness
- Courage
- Sense of humor
- Ability to be flexible
- Integrity
- Understanding
- Energy
- Creativity
- Warmth
- Resourcefulness
- Perceptiveness
- Intuitiveness
- Tenacity
- Achievement orientation
- Balance

Respondents to the HIMSS / Hersher 2002 Job Satisfaction Survey listed the skills in Figure 5-1 as those most desired to continue professional growth.

Change can be difficult, whether it's changing for a job or changing for a person. The status quo seems much easier. We tend to resist change. It means that making the transition to a new environment is difficult personally, professionally and sometimes frightening. To prepare for change and to devise a career road map, you should identify who you are. Scoring your responses to the following exercise isn't necessary. If you review your answers honestly, you will easily see where you need development.

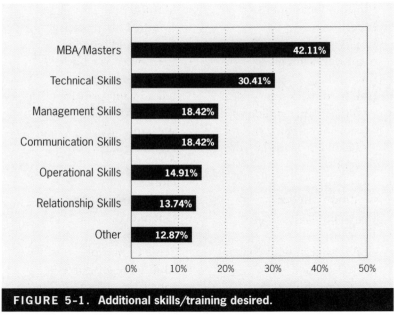

FIGURE 5-1. Additional skills/training desired.

Source: HIMSS/Hersher 2002 Job Satisfaction Survey.

SKILLS ASSESSMENT EXERCISE

1. Rate your skills and knowledge.

Even if you are satisfied with being a midlevel manager or director, be aware that CEOs are beginning to look for senior executive potential in everyone. Rate yourself in the following key leadership skills that CEOs look for across all positions:

- **Communication skills**
  - ☐ *Poor*   ☐ *Fair*   ☐ *Average*   ☐ *Good*   ☐ *Excellent*
- **Listening skills**
  - ☐ *Poor*   ☐ *Fair*   ☐ *Average*   ☐ *Good*   ☐ *Excellent*
- **Leadership / Management Experience**
  - ☐ *Poor*   ☐ *Fair*   ☐ *Average*   ☐ *Good*   ☐ *Excellent*
- **Ability to partner (both internally and externally)**
  - ☐ *Poor*   ☐ *Fair*   ☐ *Average*   ☐ *Good*   ☐ *Excellent*
- **Strategic vision**
  - ☐ *Poor*   ☐ *Fair*   ☐ *Average*   ☐ *Good*   ☐ *Excellent*
- **Team player**
  - ☐ *Poor*   ☐ *Fair*   ☐ *Average*   ☐ *Good*   ☐ *Excellent*
- **Ability to retain excellent employees with growth potential**
  - ☐ *Poor*   ☐ *Fair*   ☐ *Average*   ☐ *Good*   ☐ *Excellent*
- **Results / action oriented**
  - ☐ *Poor*   ☐ *Fair*   ☐ *Average*   ☐ *Good*   ☐ *Excellent*
- **Ability to be flexible**
  - ☐ *Poor*   ☐ *Fair*   ☐ *Average*   ☐ *Good*   ☐ *Excellent*
- **Change Agent**
  - ☐ *Poor*   ☐ *Fair*   ☐ *Average*   ☐ *Good*   ☐ *Excellent*
- **Educator**
  - ☐ *Poor*   ☐ *Fair*   ☐ *Average*   ☐ *Good*   ☐ *Excellent*
- **Entrepreneur**
  - ☐ *Poor*   ☐ *Fair*   ☐ *Average*   ☐ *Good*   ☐ *Excellent*
- **Risk Taker**
  - ☐ *Poor*   ☐ *Fair*   ☐ *Average*   ☐ *Good*   ☐ *Excellent*
- **Self-Confidence**
  - ☐ *Poor*   ☐ *Fair*   ☐ *Average*   ☐ *Good*   ☐ *Excellent*
- **Maturity**
  - ☐ *Poor*   ☐ *Fair*   ☐ *Average*   ☐ *Good*   ☐ *Excellent*
- **Comfort taking charge**
  - ☐ *Poor*   ☐ *Fair*   ☐ *Average*   ☐ *Good*   ☐ *Excellent*
- **Comfort following**
  - ☐ *Poor*   ☐ *Fair*   ☐ *Average*   ☐ *Good*   ☐ *Excellent*

- **Credibility as a leader**
  ☐ *Poor*   ☐ *Fair*   ☐ *Average*   ☐ *Good*   ☐ *Excellent*
- **Courage**
  ☐ *Poor*   ☐ *Fair*   ☐ *Average*   ☐ *Good*   ☐ *Excellent*
- **Integrity**
  ☐ *Poor*   ☐ *Fair*   ☐ *Average*   ☐ *Good*   ☐ *Excellent*
- **Sense of humor**
  ☐ *Poor*   ☐ *Fair*   ☐ *Average*   ☐ *Good*   ☐ *Excellent*
- **Ability to market new ideas**
  ☐ *Poor*   ☐ *Fair*   ☐ *Average*   ☐ *Good*   ☐ *Excellent*
- **Ability to manage relationship priorities**
  ☐ *Poor*   ☐ *Fair*   ☐ *Average*   ☐ *Good*   ☐ *Excellent*
- **Track record for delivering as promised**
  ☐ *Poor*   ☐ *Fair*   ☐ *Average*   ☐ *Good*   ☐ *Excellent*
- **Ability to hire candidates capable of carrying out the strategic vision under your direction**
  ☐ *Poor*   ☐ *Fair*   ☐ *Average*   ☐ *Good*   ☐ *Excellent*
- **Ability to be proactive**
  ☐ *Poor*   ☐ *Fair*   ☐ *Average*   ☐ *Good*   ☐ *Excellent*
- **Vulnerability**
  ☐ *Poor*   ☐ *Fair*   ☐ *Average*   ☐ *Good*   ☐ *Excellent*
- **Decisiveness**
  ☐ *Poor*   ☐ *Fair*   ☐ *Average*   ☐ *Good*   ☐ *Excellent*
- **Global view**
  ☐ *Poor*   ☐ *Fair*   ☐ *Average*   ☐ *Good*   ☐ *Excellent*
- **Coalition Builder**
  ☐ *Poor*   ☐ *Fair*   ☐ *Average*   ☐ *Good*   ☐ *Excellent*
- **Openness**
  ☐ *Poor*   ☐ *Fair*   ☐ *Average*   ☐ *Good*   ☐ *Excellent*
- **Honesty**
  ☐ *Poor*   ☐ *Fair*   ☐ *Average*   ☐ *Good*   ☐ *Excellent*
- **Understanding**
  ☐ *Poor*   ☐ *Fair*   ☐ *Average*   ☐ *Good*   ☐ *Excellent*
- **Energy**
  ☐ *Poor*   ☐ *Fair*   ☐ *Average*   ☐ *Good*   ☐ *Excellent*
- **Creativity**
  ☐ *Poor*   ☐ *Fair*   ☐ *Average*   ☐ *Good*   ☐ *Excellent*
- **Warmth**
  ☐ *Poor*   ☐ *Fair*   ☐ *Average*   ☐ *Good*   ☐ *Excellent*
- **Resourcefulness**
  ☐ *Poor*   ☐ *Fair*   ☐ *Average*   ☐ *Good*   ☐ *Excellent*

- **Perceptiveness**
  - ☐ *Poor*   ☐ *Fair*   ☐ *Average*   ☐ *Good*   ☐ *Excellent*
- **Intuitiveness**
  - ☐ *Poor*   ☐ *Fair*   ☐ *Average*   ☐ *Good*   ☐ *Excellent*
- **Tenacity**
  - ☐ *Poor*   ☐ *Fair*   ☐ *Average*   ☐ *Good*   ☐ *Excellent*
- **Achievement orientation**
  - ☐ *Poor*   ☐ *Fair*   ☐ *Average*   ☐ *Good*   ☐ *Excellent*
- **Balance**
  - ☐ *Poor*   ☐ *Fair*   ☐ *Average*   ☐ *Good*   ☐ *Excellent*
- **Image / presence / style**
  - ☐ *Poor*   ☐ *Fair*   ☐ *Average*   ☐ *Good*   ☐ *Excellent*
- **Clinical applications**
  - ☐ *Poor*   ☐ *Fair*   ☐ *Average*   ☐ *Good*   ☐ *Excellent*
- **Project management**
  - ☐ *Poor*   ☐ *Fair*   ☐ *Average*   ☐ *Good*   ☐ *Excellent*
- **Business acumen**
  - ☐ *Poor*   ☐ *Fair*   ☐ *Average*   ☐ *Good*   ☐ *Excellent*
- **Politically savvy**
  - ☐ *Poor*   ☐ *Fair*   ☐ *Average*   ☐ *Good*   ☐ *Excellent*
- **Technical knowledge**
  - ☐ *Poor*   ☐ *Fair*   ☐ *Average*   ☐ *Good*   ☐ *Excellent*
- **Negotiator**
  - ☐ *Poor*   ☐ *Fair*   ☐ *Average*   ☐ *Good*   ☐ *Excellent*
- **Financial skills (budgets, etc.)**
  - ☐ *Poor*   ☐ *Fair*   ☐ *Average*   ☐ *Good*   ☐ *Excellent*
- **Implementations**
  - ☐ *Poor*   ☐ *Fair*   ☐ *Average*   ☐ *Good*   ☐ *Excellent*
- **Presentation and public-speaking skills**
  - ☐ *Poor*   ☐ *Fair*   ☐ *Average*   ☐ *Good*   ☐ *Excellent*
- **Written communications**
  - ☐ *Poor*   ☐ *Fair*   ☐ *Average*   ☐ *Good*   ☐ *Excellent*
- **Mentoring and coaching skills**
  - ☐ *Poor*   ☐ *Fair*   ☐ *Average*   ☐ *Good*   ☐ *Excellent*
- **Planning skills**
  - ☐ *Poor*   ☐ *Fair*   ☐ *Average*   ☐ *Good*   ☐ *Excellent*
- **Sales skills**
  - ☐ *Poor*   ☐ *Fair*   ☐ *Average*   ☐ *Good*   ☐ *Excellent*
- **Ability to deal with changes**
  - ☐ *Poor*   ☐ *Fair*   ☐ *Average*   ☐ *Good*   ☐ *Excellent*

Before jumping into your career plan take a few more minutes and answer the open-ended questions. These are part of the skill assessment and are things for you to think about.

2. List all previous positions with
    ☐ Dates
    ☐ Responsibilities
    ☐ Accomplishments
    ☐ Reason for leaving
    ☐ What you liked and disliked about each job

3. List all other pertinent experience
    ☐ Schooling
    ☐ Professional organizations
    ☐ Public speaking
    ☐ Volunteer activities
    ☐ Sports
    ☐ Government
    ☐ Interests and hobbies

4. Which positions have you enjoyed the most? Why?

5. (a) Which projects did you find the most enjoyable? Why?

    (b) Which projects would you never do again? Why?

6. What type of environment is most comfortable for you (entrepreneurial, for-profit, not-for-profit, large, small, etc.)? What environment do you like the best?

7. (a) How would you rate your people-management skills?
    ☐ Excellent
    ☐ Good
    ☐ Average
    ☐ Fair
    ☐ Poor

    (b) Do you enjoy managing people?
    ☐ Yes   ☐ No

8. (a) How would you rate your project-management skills?
    ☐ Excellent
    ☐ Good
    ☐ Average
    ☐ Fair
    ☐ Poor

    (b) Do you enjoy managing projects?
    ☐ Yes   ☐ No

9. What kind of projects do you enjoy?

10. What applications do you know well?

11. What are your long-term career goals?

12. Based on your ratings and evaluation, what skills do you need to acquire or improve in the short-term?

Develop a plan to acquire these important skills through:
- Education and training
- Experience
- Mentoring
- Professional associations

After completing your skills assessment, focus on evaluating both your current position and previous positions that you may have held. Evaluate and catalogue the things that you enjoy as well as those you dislike. For each entry, ask yourself why you feel the way you do.

Almost any position requires appropriate soft skills, whether you are a project leader, a director, or an aspiring CIO. Some of these skills you possess innately and some you learn through experience, maturity, mentoring and concerted effort. Hard skills, or measurable skills, may be slightly easier to identify or acquire, but not always.

As an example, a skill that is important for long-term success—yet terrifying for most people—is public speaking. If you have never spoken before a group, you first need to identify what worries you and get advice from someone who is a good public speaker. Ask that person what makes his or her speeches successful.

Then proceed slowly. Volunteer to conduct an in-service program at work and ask your boss to critique you, the content and the presentation. Do the same thing for a larger group. Then, if you are successful, apply to be a guest speaker for your local Healthcare Information and Management Systems Society (HIMSS) chapter or user group. The more you speak, the more comfortable you will become—as long as you are willing to take criticism. Public speaking is a learned skill and one that combines many of the soft skills mentioned earlier.

Use the same methodology with any of the skills you want to acquire. Acquiring new skills takes time, trial and error and a great deal of self-discipline. Many of the soft skills outlined in this chapter are inside all of us; we just need to give them a chance to surface and mature.

GROWTH POTENTIAL IN YOUR ORGANIZATION

Now that you've assessed your skills, it's time to assess your IT growth potential within your current organization. Here are some key questions that you will need to ask yourself:

- Have I been given special projects?
- Have I been promoted in the past?
- Have I been considered for other positions?
- Does my organization have a track record of promoting from within?
- Are there established career ladders?
- Have I been exposed to other departments?
- Have I been given adequate educational opportunities?
- Have I approached my boss about advancement, and was he or she encouraging and supportive?
- Does my boss discuss important issues with me?
- Have I exhausted all internal options?
- Have I lost power?
- Am I being left out of meetings?
- Has my boss lost power?

CHAPTER 6

The Importance of Mentoring, Coaching and Leadership

We all need to continue growing, regardless of where we are in our careers. Take on new challenges and embrace new ideas, new peers, new mentors and new initiatives. Don't be afraid to volunteer for new assignments. Doing so will prove to your organization that you are happy to be there and committed to producing quality results. Focus on continually improving your leadership skills.

THE ROLE OF MENTORS AND COACHES

Identifying and working with a strong mentor is critical to continued growth and development. Most of us need to work with a variety of mentors, perhaps one for leadership, one for project management and another for presentations. Astutely selecting people that you respect and asking for their help and advice is a positive way to ensure your continued growth.

Succession planning is new to the healthcare industry. When Lee Iaccoca, chairman of Chrysler Corporation was ready to retire, he had three people in line to take his place. How is this relevant to healthcare? It isn't relevant at all. It has only been recently that the healthcare world has seriously looked at succession planning. Particularly as it relates to the non-IT ranks, we are still reluctant to put in a successor to a CEO. For example, consider a COO who for years has done a very good job and has all but been promised the CEO position when the CEO retires. As mentioned previously in Chapter 5, when a senior officer steps down i.e., retires, there would be an immediate phone call to one of their old cronies from graduate school. So with that in place, why would we need mentors and coaches if no one believed in succession planning?

In the last few years—particularly given a significant change in the healthcare marketplace and after Y2K was successfully managed—IT departments were seen as heroes. We are now back to running our healthcare systems. CIOs began to take a very serious look at succession planning. It is important to ensure that their successors have been fully educated in budgeting and planning and exposed to the executive team when the bosses retire. This isn't an easy process. It takes a great deal of planning and thinking in order to ensure that the CIOs' successors will be accepted. Interestingly enough, now that the healthcare industry has done its job and there are successors in place, it only works about half the time, and failure often occurs within the first year. However, half is better than none. So how do you become a CIO successor? Do you hold on for three or four years until your boss / trainer resigns?

Finding mentors and coaches is one of the most critical things that a potential successor can do. The screening process for mentors and coaches should be taken seriously. Know what to expect from your mentor or coach. Good mentors are people that you admire and would like to emulate and learn from. They are typically successful in their professions and well respected by their organizations. Approach potential mentors and let them know that you want to learn from them. Ask for a commitment and promise to make a commitment yourself in return.

DIFFERENCE BETWEEN A MENTOR AND A COACH

There is a definite difference between a mentor and a coach. A mentor serves a very important role for you; they do indeed open doors and tell you where the landmines are. They check in with you from time to time, and you should check in with them. Seeking out a coach, however, is more important. Your coach watches your progress and makes course corrections. The types of coaches you need may vary based on the particular challenges that you are facing. If you are managing your first major implementation, seek coaches who have been there, done that successfully. A coach needs to be tough, and you need to listen. A coach might be internal, external or someone you hire. Your coach may be a family member, a colleague from a professional organization or even your boss.

Finding a good coach who has the time for you, however, is difficult. You will both be giving up a great deal of time and shared goals in order to make the coaching role successful. In particular, finding a coach who has the time to work with you, who you trust enough to critique some of your actions and who you feel comfortable being open and honest with is the challenge.

Figure 6-1 summarizes how respondents to the HIMSS / Hersher 2002 Job Satisfaction Survey evaluated their supervisors. Figure 6-2 identifies the skills that survey respondents felt they needed from a good coach or mentor.

Conversely, as we progress in our careers, it is our responsibility to share our skills and insights with others as they strive to progress and grow. Repay the favors you have received from others by providing the mentoring needed by more junior associates in the industry. Without committed, viable mentors and coaches who are willing to share their lessons learned, our leaders and managers of the future will progress at a much slower pace.

Management and leadership are often considered to go hand-in-hand. We tend to assume that to be a good leader, a person must also be a good manager. Although that is an ideal scenario, the truth is that exceptional leaders aren't necessarily good managers and vice versa.

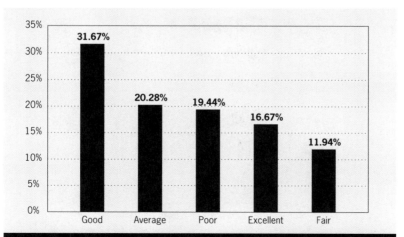

FIGURE 6-1. Evaluating supervisors as mentors/coaches.

Source: HIMSS/Hersher 2002 Job Satisfaction Survey.

DEFINING WHAT A LEADER SHOULD BE

Leadership is essential to the successful completion of any project. Without it, activities flounder and frequently take the wrong course. No matter how simple or complex the project or the organization, someone must take charge and set the direction.

What exactly is leadership? Leadership is an art. It isn't an exact science. Leadership is the ability to create a vision of where an organization or project needs to go and to sell that vision to the decision makers and to those who must work to make the vision a reality. Just as management skills are identified and learned at an early age, leadership is an ability that is both innate and learned. It requires confidence in your ability and judgment and a willingness to put yourself at risk. Leadership requires emotional maturity, whatever your age. Leadership can and should change with the situation. Good leaders are also comfortable with vulnerability, have learned from their failures, and are comfortable saying "I don't know."

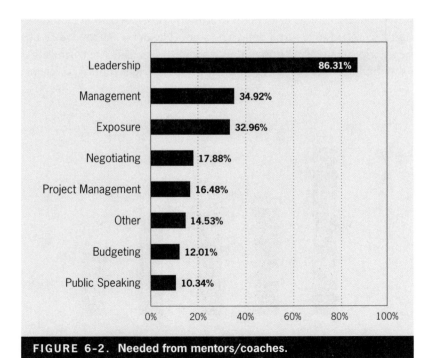

FIGURE 6-2. Needed from mentors/coaches.

Source: HIMSS/Hersher 2002 Job Satisfaction Survey.

Does everyone need leadership to be successful in his or her careers? The answer, to a certain degree, is yes. If we always wait to be directed and never take the initiative to move forward, the odds are that success will elude us. Recognize that there is a need for leadership in everything we do. Something as simple as determining how to commemorate the end of an implementation requires someone to recognize that it should be celebrated. They must then decide what the celebration should involve, sell the idea to their boss and to the people who must plan the party and make it happen. Clearly there are many of us who prefer not to take a visible leadership role. That's okay if you aren't in a position that requires visibility. Don't misinterpret visibility with the ability to lead quietly and consistently.

Do you always have to take the lead? Quite the opposite, and if you are required or feel the need to take the lead in every situation, you are in for a lot of conflict. Teamwork and an appreciation of differing ideas and visions are crucial. The most successful executives in all industries know when to take the lead and when to defer to someone else. Taking the lead, even in very small projects, will help you develop confidence and ability. Contrary to popular belief, leadership can be learned.

How do you know if you're a good leader? Look at the results of projects where you took a leadership role. Did you accomplish your vision? Did your organization feel good about the results? Did you? Were you able to adapt and change course as obstacles developed? Did you keep your goal in your own mind and in the minds of others? Did you seek counsel when you needed it?

If you answered yes to all of the preceding questions, you have great leadership skills. If you answered no to a few, you know where you need growth and improvement.

What are some examples of your ability to lead? Leadership skills are something that begin to develop early in life and continue to grow as we mature and are exposed to new situations. Sometimes we ask to take the leadership role and, at other times, it is thrust upon us. Sometimes leadership is born of necessity. Think back over the various leadership roles that you have played and evaluate when you were most successful and why. You may be surprised to learn that you were successful even when the role was thrust upon you.

As you assess your skills, attributes and career objectives, don't overlook the critical importance of leadership experience. Push yourself to assume leadership roles whenever possible. Learn from your mistakes.

Identify individuals that you consider to be good leaders. Observe them. Ask to work closely with them on projects. Learn from them.

Remember, without good leadership, tremendous amounts of effort are often wasted.

THE NEED FOR GOOD LEADERS

The need for well-rounded leaders has never been greater. Advances in technology have boomed in recent years, and their effects on healthcare continue to evolve. Change management, resource management and flexibility are the keys to success in a chaotic healthcare environment. Leading others through turbulent and often murky waters sometimes seems to call for a special kind of leader.

Take an active role in leading the changes in your organization. Communicate those changes clearly and consistently. Support and encourage others in your organization. Foster sensitivity and patience, but set clear goals for yourself and others. Follow through on those goals.

Change requires patience and an environment that views change as a positive opportunity. A leader must be fully capable of articulating the need for change and making decisions in a steady and efficient manner.

Demonstrating your leadership skills is only one of many ways to experience growth in your position. Go above and beyond the call of duty to make a name for yourself. Do innovative research or create new solutions. Your boss will be pleased if you take a problem off his or her plate, so get involved.

Think about other ways to get more deeply involved in your healthcare profession. Join organizations, read industry periodicals or volunteer to represent your department at user group meetings. Such experiences give you increased exposure and broaden your awareness of things you want to do as you develop and grow into your new job. If you aren't getting the information you need to succeed, or if you aren't getting the opportunities you want, you have to go after them.

CHAPTER 7

Nonhealthcare Professionals: Making the Transition into the Healthcare Environment

The healthcare industry has long been considered a special club for members only, meaning that you had to be experienced in healthcare if you wanted to find a job in the industry. This notion has changed in IT areas as well as other departments. For some time, CEOs have been strongly considering nonhealthcare candidates for finance and marketing positions.

So, why has the healthcare industry recognized the need for professionals with nonhealthcare backgrounds? Why are we now more open to considering a wider range of experiences?

Healthcare organizations are devising plans to prepare for the future. As baby boomers enter retirement, patient care needs to become more efficient, more comprehensive, more progressive and more technical. The industry needs growth and expansion into new areas, which is why nonhealthcare, nontraditional professionals are so highly sought by some healthcare organizations.

Issues such as rising costs, competition and more limited reimbursement are forcing organizations to be more aggressive, creative and resourceful than ever before. Healthcare organizations can learn from the experiences of other industries such as manufacturing, transportation and financial services that may have gone through similar challenges.

Many powerful stakeholders within healthcare, not to mention government, are pushing us further and faster than ever before. This may be an excellent time for more broadly based IT professionals or executives to enter our market. Sophisticated new technologies are available to healthcare organizations today, yet few experienced healthcare IT people have the required level of expertise with the new technology and security systems. The various constituents who play important roles in the delivery of care and the business side of healthcare are uniquely different and more complex than those in the nonhealthcare world.

The areas from where nonhealthcare candidates are emerging include supply chain management, hotel services, e-commerce, security and privacy. In some cases, the chairman of the board steps in as CEO when the role is vacated. Some of these interim CEOs stay on permanently and can be very effective, particularly if they forge a trusting relationship with the clinical team. Not only are board members from industry stepping into healthcare CEO roles, but they are also pressuring and demanding that healthcare CEOs run their organizations more like businesses and draw upon executive talent that will bring new ideas to healthcare.

This isn't to say that there aren't enough healthcare candidates. It simply means that some of the roles can easily be filled by nontraditional candidates who have the experience healthcare organizations are seeking.

There has been a major influx of candidates with military backgrounds who now wish to enter the private sector healthcare industry. In terms of technology, the military is probably the most advanced sector. But there are far more benefits. Experienced IT professionals with significant military careers are retiring, eager to share their knowledge and experience with the private sector. Given the educational support that the military offers, many healthcare IT professionals have gone on to complete multiple and advanced degrees. This creates a well-educated, experienced talent pool.

Not everyone can make the jump from the military side. Conversely, hiring military experts isn't always acceptable because of old prejudices. Before we talk about the prejudices against military candidates, it is important to deal with the positive attitude first. A positive aspect of considering a military candidate—especially if they are leaving before their 20-year retirement—is that they may have been given significantly more responsibility at a younger age than their healthcare IT peers. A common military practice is to move very good candidates back and forth from staff jobs to large management jobs.

It is very difficult for a layperson to understand their background.

Therefore, some old prejudices come marching out, such as a military person is rigid, understands the chain of command and will not deviate from it and will not take orders from outside the chain of command. Others may also question how a military person makes decisions and how creative they are—having come from the military when jobs are assured.

In addition, it is sometimes thought that military candidates simply can't understand civilian or private sector healthcare, particularly as it relates to IT. However, it's important to point out that the Department of Defense and the Veterans Administration have had some of the best healthcare systems in the country over the last ten years. Out of necessity, as their personnel move from location to location, it becomes critical to have an electronic health record and a very active data repository.

Unfortunately, many very well qualified military candidates are never given an opportunity because of their background. This puts them in an extremely untenable position, as we need an influx of IT executives at all levels into the civilian world. What a shame to eliminate the use of our fine military personnel.

INFLUENCES ON HIRING NONHEALTHCARE CANDIDATES

In recent years, two significant factors have influenced the hiring of nonhealthcare candidates into healthcare IT positions.

Shortly before Y2K, we experienced recruitment and retention problems stemming from the movement of IT experts into non-healthcare arenas; these professionals were being actively recruited by other industries. As Y2K approached, the healthcare industry experienced a great demand to bring in the very best IT executives. Interestingly, a large number of chief technology officers (CTOs), directors of technology and other technology-focused personnel were recruited from outside healthcare and weren't developed or promoted internally.

An even more important factor was that individuals with non-healthcare backgrounds had the capabilities to succeed in many of the new healthcare IT positions created post–Y2K.

Positions opened up in critical areas, and they required broad-based technology, project management and application expertise. As the industry continues to evolve, healthcare organizations have discovered that many traditional IT management positions—as well as new roles in security, privacy and customer service—don't require healthcare experience.

Specific positions where nonhealthcare IT professionals can make easy transitions into healthcare include chief technology officer, director of technology, manager or director of networks or telecommunications and security officer, as well as many lower-level technology roles. Positions where customer service plays a key role might do well for nonhealthcare candidates. The office of project management can easily be filled by an experienced nonhealthcare candidate.

Transitioning into CIO or director of applications positions is harder to accomplish for nonhealthcare IT professionals. Enterprise resource planning (ERP) positions offer the easiest transition for people from other industries experienced with systems such as People-Soft or Lawson.

For nonhealthcare candidates to successfully transition into the healthcare environment, it isn't as daunting as it might seem. They will succeed if they demonstrate their skills and knowledge base. They also need to immerse themselves in the environment and clearly understand the power base. Physicians not respecting non-healthcare IT is a myth. Physicians respect knowledge and credibility. Learning to adapt to a new corporate culture, somewhat obscure power players and the politics in a very complex healthcare environment is much more challenging than learning the technology.

The healthcare industry is more complex than most and continues to be one of the top two industries hiring even during these turbulent times. Candidates with nonhealthcare backgrounds can bring new perspectives to an organization. IT executives can have years of success in other industries, but adapting to fit the unique healthcare environment can be far more challenging than one might expect.

Fairly recently, senior-level healthcare managers have begun to realize the mission-critical nature of data and technology. Such data and technology not only impacts the running of a healthcare business but also the future success of patient care and clinical redesign, as healthcare business increasingly leaves the hospital and enters the outpatient arena. In response, the healthcare industry has opened its doors to nonhealthcare professionals, due primarily to the skills and new perspectives they bring to the table.

More nonhealthcare IT professionals are trying to transition into healthcare today than ever before. The poor economy, loss of jobs and candidates' desire for stability make the healthcare industry seem very attractive today.

SPECIAL SKILLS NEEDED IN HEALTHCARE IT

What special skills do you need to be successful in a healthcare IT environment?

Of course, the most important skill is the skill you've been hired for. Some additional skills you will need to achieve your goals include:

- Understanding and respecting the mission of healthcare.
- Understanding the various power bases such as physicians and clinicians is crucial to success.
- Having knowledge of unique healthcare IT vendors and their products.
- Maintaining a cutting edge, dynamic outlook on IT.
- Being flexible in your thinking.
- Adapting a strong business style and demonstrating sound decision-making skills and actions.
- Understanding your role as an executive capable of bridging the gap between business and healthcare.
- Learning the political landscape.
- Communicating often and clearly.

While you adapt to the healthcare environment, there are certain attitudes you must avoid. For example, you will need to reject the temptation to say things like, "At Motorola, we used to do it this way." The contributions you make need to be done in a subtle, businesslike manner.

The healthcare industry is operating as a business. You need to be innovative, financially savvy and politically astute. Feedback and opinions from various stakeholders should be heard and understood before starting a new project. Understanding what may be very differing opinions can be overwhelming for someone who is new to healthcare. In terms of policy, procedure and influence, many issues need to be addressed to ensure successful projects. This applies particularly in academic medical centers, where the mission encompasses patient care, education and research.

Growth in the healthcare industry is unlimited. As we enter a new era that finally recognizes the critical nature of the healthcare IT organization as it affects the enterprise and the future growth of diverse entities, we are more and more open to individuals who offer a broad background. New technology is making possible many of the initiatives that were either too costly or too difficult in the past.

If you're hired in November as the CTO, don't expect to be named CIO in January. A year is probably the minimum amount of time you will need to get up to speed, gain the trust of the clinical community and recognize the unlimited number of career opportunities.

Overall, to be successful in any healthcare IT enterprise, you need to exhibit the skills of an expert and be adaptable to the corporate culture you are serving.

CHAPTER 8

Internal Promotions: Making Them Happen

I t is important to note that career development doesn't mean that you have to uproot yourself from your current organization to pursue opportunities elsewhere. As part of the interview process for your current job, your potential was assessed. Before you jump too quickly to a new job, work with your mentor or boss and inquire about other opportunities within your organization. The challenges and opportunities you seek could be right under your nose. You've already put in a lot of time and effort with your current employer, so we recommend building on that success internally before exploring opportunities externally.

As a professional, you must properly assess many issues to determine your potential for receiving an internal promotion. For example, do your superiors do succession planning, which ultimately means that they groom managers, directors and others to receive promotions and assume new responsibilities? In addition, you must consider your loyalty and your organization's loyalty. Do you respect your boss and your employer? Do they respect you? Can you enlist them in your career growth? This should have been assessed before you took your job, but the opportunity for growth can change rapidly. The culture can change with the board or executive changes (see Chapter 10).

THE INTERVIEW PROCESS

Your ability to receive an internal promotion is determined by several factors. The first factor is the person who hires you—your boss. When you are interviewing, one of your questions should be, "How will I progress in the organization?" And the interviewer will probably ask, "What are you looking for?"

You want to join an organization that believes in the growth and development of their internal talent. So, during the interview process, the first step in evaluating an organization is to ask yourself, "Can I stay here and continue to grow or will I have to go elsewhere?" This, of course, becomes a really serious issue if you are continually moving your family from one new location to another. If something doesn't feel right during the interview process, you may need to consider declining the job offer and going elsewhere.

If you aren't comfortable during the first interview, you need to probe more deeply to determine why. Ask your potential boss what his or her career progression has been in this particular organization. Then find out how many IT managers have been promoted from within.

One way to get additional information, particularly if you are being looked at for a management role, is to find out how many individuals will report to you and what their development has been like. A simple way to get to that issue is to ask the interviewer three questions:

- What is your retention strategy / succession plan?
- Is there a budget for outside education?
- What has been your turnover in the IT organization in the last five years?

Interestingly enough, the third question is tricky. Do you personally prefer higher turnover or lower turnover? For instance, if you're told that the longevity in the IT organization is 10 to 20 years, you may want to scratch your head and wonder how people have grown or why they've stayed in the same positions for all those years. Have the people stayed because the organization encourages internal growth and promotes from within, or has the entire senior management team been stagnant?

The answer you would like to hear is that the people have stayed because they've received multiple promotions. Interestingly enough, that is generally not the case. They stay because they are comfortable, not necessarily because they have grown. You need to pursue that issue. Be direct and ask.

At times, it's not a bad idea for a manager to combat complacency by bringing in some outside talent. A good leader will have a balance of new hires and individuals that he or she has been able to train or promote.

Another way to find out about internal promotions is to ask:
- What do you expect of me?
- What factors will you consider in determining whether I'm someone who should be promoted?
- What benchmarks do you look for?

You need to hear thoughtful responses to these questions.

Among the hardest questions to ask during an interview—and among the most risky if you ask them too soon—are, "What traits do you see in me that make you think I could be a good member of your organization? Given the brief amount of time we've had to talk, what are some skills or characteristics you have seen that I would benefit from working on?"

Another tricky question that must be timed very well and must not be seen as a threat by the person you are speaking with would be, "What are your aspirations and how have they been supported by your manager?"

One of the most important ways to determine your growth potential is to assess the corporate culture. Find out if the overall corporate culture is very different from the culture in IT. Ideally, you would want the two cultures to be parallel. Bringing up the subject of cultures will highlight any "we versus they" attitudes and can be very dangerous. After all, the powers that be may not want to approve too many internal promotions because they may hope to bring new blood into the IT division by hiring externally. Again, we want to emphasize that many of these issues can and should be explored during the interview process, as they should play a major role in your decision to accept a job offer.

Beware if you are going into an organizational culture that doesn't feel right to you. (We will discuss this issue in depth in a later chapter.) If you are uncomfortable but confident that things will change, think again. If you will be working for a boss who has a few idiosyncrasies that you're positive you can deal with, or if you're thinking that your boss will change and that some of your great ideas will help move the organization forward, think again. Taking such a job is like marrying someone who you're sure will change his or her habits just because you want them to.

The best way to grow and get the chance to tackle a new role is to look within your current organization, where you already have coaches and mentors that know your abilities. Because people within your current organization already know you, if a new opportunity comes along, they may be more willing to let you take a shot at it, even if you don't meet all the requirements outlined in the formal job description. Very often, internal promotions are highly successful because the people around you want to see you succeed and will do everything they can to expose you to new opportunities for growth.

At times, you may feel pushed. At times, you may feel that you can't do the job. That's when you need to turn to your coach or mentor and ask for help. Of course, you may also encounter a backlash from time to time. You get promoted, but the response isn't totally positive. Some of your peers may be supportive, and some may be jealous. It takes a lot of wisdom and leadership to manage former peers.

One key indicator that you need to begin to look for growth, either internally or externally, is your strong desire to be challenged and do something different. Another key indicator is boredom. Are you busy enough to not watch the clock? The most important factors are your energy level and desire to succeed. A good measure of job enthusiasm and energy is whether you enjoy walking in the front door of work every day. If you miss an internal promotion for good reason, find out what you can do better next time. Don't give up if you have an excellent boss. He or she will give you the opportunity to grow because he or she can't grow unless you grow.

On the other hand, it is ill advised to take an internal promotion that you know isn't good for you just because it's offered, especially if you are tempted to settle for the job because you cannot or will not relocate. You could fail and then where would you be? Examine your motivations carefully. Either stay where you are until something more appropriate comes along, look elsewhere in your region for openings that would make you happy or ask for additional projects or responsibilities that will allow you to grow.

SUCCESSION PLANNING

Healthcare organizations have historically been remiss in encouraging succession planning. For example, very few COOs went on to become CEOs, and if people wanted growth, they generally had to leave. However, things have changed somewhat in the last few years. We are seeing some successors being given jobs on an interim basis but not always for the right reasons. Sometimes the executive attitude is, "Let's give them a chance for a year, and if it does not work, we will consider hiring from the outside." Hiring a successor who is not quite ready for his or her boss' job without hiring a coach to support them is probably a mistake. At the end of the year, if the successor does not "make it," salary dollars may have been saved, but a hopeful CIO may be discouraged and, all in all, it's been a lose-lose situation for everyone.

As we look more specifically into the IT marketplace, we see that only recently have CIOs begun preparing the next generation of IT leaders to take over, and only recently have they had the money to do so. It takes time to train people and strategically align them with the executive team so they will be accepted as leaders when they are ready to take over a higher role.

CIOs and IT directors and managers must prepare for the future of their organization and the overall industry by identifying and developing the second generation of IT leadership. So, what do they look for when they assess you as a professional?

- Leadership skills
- Mentoring and coaching abilities
- Business skills
- Communication skills
- Commitment to the organization
- Team-playing skills
- Project-management skills

Truly, there is no emphasis on specific technical skills. Instead, those who assess your skills look at the big picture. They do not look for specialists or one-dimensional professionals. Instead, they look at your performance in a broad range of areas, including how you communicate with peers, superiors and subordinates; how you communicate and negotiate when asked to manage projects and tasks; how well you understand concepts related to business development, finance and marketing in addition to IT topics; and how strong your commitment to the organization is.

Excellent succession planning, which includes loyalty, exposure, mentoring and development, is critical not only to your organization, but to the industry as a whole. Developing capable new leaders is essential to the future success of healthcare IT organizations.

LOYALTY

Your commitment (that is, your loyalty) can speak volumes about your career goals. Loyalty should not be transitory or linked to one person. Loyalty grows over a period of time and is built on trust. If trust has been built, just because your boss has a bad day, you have a bad day or the assignment you receive is not a good one, your loyalty will not diminish. Loyalty requires patience and respect. In our current healthcare environment, the challenges that confront all of us test our loyalty and trust on a daily basis.

We have found that more and more employees are looking forward to staying in one environment longer than they have in the past. They believe they can grow and develop there because it has become a safe haven. The environment supplies situations in which employees gain respect and self-esteem while growing and being challenged through their work.

The days of employees frequently changing jobs just to achieve higher salaries and better titles are slowly slipping away. They are being replaced by issues related to quality of personal life and work life. To support such quality of life issues, a very strong relationship needs to develop between employees and their employers. These relationships need to be tied more and more to mutual respect and less and less to a paycheck.

Loyalty takes us through thick and thin, long hours and times when loved ones are in trouble and we need help from our colleagues. It encourages us to do more than just our job. It encourages us to help our peers and support our boss, customers and the goals and mission of our organization. Respect, loyalty and pride in one's workplace go hand-in-hand.

Achieving loyalty between yourself and your boss, peers and subordinates does not happen overnight. It is a long process built on cooperating, compromising, setting aside one's own needs, and stepping forward and taking charge when projects require it.

How do you recognize an environment where loyalty is rewarded? There are many signs to look for. Ask yourself these questions:

- Can you have honest and open dialogue with your peers and your boss?
- Can you objectively talk through problems?
- Can you set deadlines and priorities that support you, your project, the people that work for you and your boss?
- Are you able to make compromises to address problems?
- Do you feel that you are working on a team that makes you want to do your very best?
- Are mistakes supported? Is it a risk-taking environment? Are you allowed to experiment? Can you be entrepreneurial? Are you rewarded for all of the preceding behaviors? Are you rewarded for mistakes?

A good coach will use the opportunity presented by a mistake to train and develop you, so that the next time you are faced with a similar situation, you will succeed. That is someone who is loyal, someone who trusts you and someone who you, in turn, can trust.

In the best cases, CIOs and other executives focus on identifying the best talent they can find and developing it, knowing that the individuals will both make them look good and build a more solid organization. Some of the best CIOs in the country take pride in this accomplishment. Frequently, they call us to say that they have developed a successor who is ready to be a CIO in his or her own right. Often this occurs when the CIO is not planning to move on but wants his or her successor to continue to grow.

As a job or promotion seeker, you must understand your environment. If you're seeking new opportunities or challenges, ask for them. If you've been with your organization long enough and have done your job well, there is no reason why you should not get the promotion. You've earned it.

WHEN NOT TO LOOK FOR A JOB

Sometimes we begin looking for a new job for all of the wrong reasons. The decision to make a job change should never be a knee-jerk reaction. Here are some of the many wrong reasons for changing positions.

Someone New Is Put in a Position over You. Do not assume that this is necessarily a bad thing. You may need more experience to be ready for that position yourself. Look to the new individual as someone you can learn from. Make sure the person knows that you would like his or her mentorship. Be positive and helpful. In response, your new boss may well appreciate your positive team attitude and reward you with growth opportunities.

A New Executive Team Is Hired. Do not panic. Perhaps a new team has been brought in to turn things around. Financial restraints and fierce competition may require a change in leadership. Give the situation time to play out. Be flexible and adaptable.

You're Assigned to a Bad Project That You Do Not Want to Do. Before you give up, see if you can change your assignment. Perhaps there is something else for you to work on that is equally important. If not, accept that the project will be over in a specific period of time and learn everything you can from the experience.

You Have Not Exhausted All Possible Avenues for Growth within Your Current Organization. Aggressively pursue growth internally. Articulate your interests and need for growth. Ask to be assigned to projects that will foster growth. Turn over every single stone to find opportunities for growth. It is always better to be promoted into new opportunities. This demonstrates success in a career.

You Are Getting Pressure from Friends and Family. Sometimes friends and family think they know what is best for you. Only you can know if you need to change positions. Make sure you understand their perspective and really agree with what they are saying before you listen to their advice. Be realistic.

A Checklist of Pros and Cons Says It's Time to Move On. A decision to move on must also be based on gut and intuition. Not all factors are equal. Only you can know how the elements of your decision should be weighted. Trust your intuition and really pay attention if any of the following negatives arise and cannot be changed:
- Despite your efforts, you are no longer challenged.
- You cannot find growth internally.
- You do not feel respected.
- You are blocked for promotion.
- You are no longer invited to key meetings.
- Your opinion is not solicited.
- Others are being promoted around you.
- You do not get the education and training you need.

Timing is everything. There will be times during your professional development when you firmly believe that accepting a new opportunity will be most advantageous to your career. Trust your intuition, but be aware of the world around you. Maintain a professional perspective, because you will encounter instances when holding on to what you have could lead to something exciting and perhaps unexpected.

If you truly believe that you have exhausted all avenues and if it is apparent that you cannot possibly develop your career within your current organization, you know it is time to explore opportunities elsewhere.

CHAPTER 9

Marketing Yourself

Marketing is a mystery, and to most of us, something that's unappealing. I am who I am, so why do I need to package myself? It seems phony.

However, marketing yourself does not mean that you can't present yourself as who you truly are or that you need to change your personal style or fudge on your background. When you are looking for a new job, marketing yourself is simply presenting yourself and your accomplishments in the best light.

To market yourself, you need to become comfortable with yourself, as well as with both your accomplishments and your weaknesses. Many of us tend to dwell on the negatives more easily than the positives. If that includes you, try to find a balance before marketing yourself—whether within your organization or outside. Marketing means something very different to each of us, but the first thing that often comes to mind is the need to be flashy or to create a story that strays ever so slightly from the truth.

As a job seeker, you have one opportunity to make a first impression. Once you make a good impression, you have an opportunity to further your job inquiry. Your first point of contact is your resume, which must be created as an extremely well done marketing document. Your second point of contact is your interview, which is probably your most powerful opportunity to make a positive impression. Clearly, the credentials listed on your resume will get you that interview. Most of your interviewing success will come down to matching the corporate culture, expressing your personal style, and communicating clearly and directly.

Perhaps this is the first time you've actually had to sell yourself. If so, assess your marketing comfort by asking yourself the following questions:

- Do you know your skills?
- Are you comfortable sharing your accomplishments?
- Are you proud of yourself? Are other people proud of you?

Other people should be seen only as verifiers of what you already know about yourself. More simply put, if you don't feel proud of your own accomplishments, no one can feel proud of them for you. Probably even more important to your career growth is the flip side of the coin: if you aren't comfortable with whom you are or aspire to be, you will find it very difficult to receive constructive criticism.

RESUME WRITING: MARKETING YOURSELF ON PAPER

A good place to start on the marketing process is to draft a resume. As you embark on your career journey, the most important marketing tool you have is probably your resume. The form and substance of your resume will create the first impression employers have of you, well before they ever put a face with your name. That is why your resume must present a thorough, accurate, and polished list of credentials. If your resume doesn't make a dynamic first impression, it is unlikely that employers will ever meet with you. Your resume and a strong cover letter open the door to meeting with potential employers.

Because you have already assessed your skills, you should be ready to begin drafting your resume. In addition, you will want to review your career path document to make sure you incorporate elements that will help you achieve the goal you have set. As an example, if your goal is to be a director of clinical systems and you're already an experienced and highly respected project manager, it would be smart to include every piece of clinical experience you have, no matter how minimal. Your project management skills and some clinical experience might move you to the head of the line and get you an interview. From there, you're on your own.

We will share some general information and some ideas about resumes. Because this very important marketing document is your first introduction to a company, it needs to project a profile of who you are, not just the bare facts. Your personality should be easily discernable in the tone of your resume and cover letter.

When we are working with excellent candidates but they aren't getting through the front door, in most cases, it is their resumes that hinder them. If they rewrite them appropriately, interviews usually follow.

Your resume should begin with the present and go reverse chronologically. First impressions are important. Often employers reject resumes if they appear sloppy or are poorly written. Be sure to list dates and locations for each position, but group all positions with the same company under one master heading with the total number of years. You want your resume to clearly reflect that you aren't a job-hopper but someone who has progressed and held different responsibilities for the same employer.

Even though many organizations will request that you submit your resume via e-mail, printed copies are still a necessity. Resumes should be printed on high-quality, white or off-white paper. Unusual colors aren't recommended. If your resume is more than one page, be sure to include your name, address, phone number(s), and e-mail address on each page, just in case the pages become separated.

After your demographics, write a brief summary paragraph about your experience and skills. It is not a good idea to list your objective or desired positions because such information will not always be appropriate. Focus on who you are, not what you want to be.

Do not misrepresent education, such as listing the number of years you attended college instead of specifying a degree. You should list things such as military service, special language skills and hobbies. First, they show a personal side of you. Second, something in your background may establish common ground with your interviewer. Personal information should be minimal and listed at the end. If you have numerous presentations or publications, you may want to consider listing them in a separate addendum to your resume.

Writing a resume can be a very intimidating task. You can get advice from the numerous books that have been written on the subject, consultants who specialize in creating the perfect document and your coworkers, friends and relatives. The unfortunate truth, however, is that if you ask three different sources, you will probably get three very different answers.

As a result, many people postpone drafting their resume indefinitely or until it becomes urgent because a headhunter has called or they have heard about a position they would like to pursue. To help you avoid rushing to put something together under pressure, we advocate that you take the time to periodically develop your resume. We also recommend that you maintain a file documenting your accomplishments so that you don't draw a blank when writing or updating your resume.

You will also save time and avoid trouble if you update your resume at least once a year to incorporate changes in job, title and demographic information, as well as accomplishments and responsibilities since your last draft. This process also allows you to reflect on your growth and whether your career is on target with your plan.

It is a particularly good idea to update your resume about a month before your annual review. You will go into the review better prepared and more able to speak to your accomplishments and discuss your goals for the future.

Resumes should be very clear and concise. They should reflect your significant accomplishments—not just your responsibilities. Let people know what you have achieved, including awards and other special recognition. If you are managing people, budgets and projects, be sure to include that information.

We recommend that you always show military service, if applicable. Be sure to include unique or extraordinary experiences, such as time spent in other countries. In addition to detailing your work experience, your resume should paint a complete picture of your interests and who you are.

Typos and errors are deadly. Be sure to proof and proof again and then ask others you respect to review the document for content and errors.

Never include your picture or be too cutesy. Make sure that hard copies are printed on a good-quality printer. Never print more than 100 copies if you are having them professionally done, as inevitably, you will later see things you want to change.

The purpose of a resume is to help you sell yourself and your skills to recruiters and prospective employers. Developing a great resume takes time and effort, but it is well worth the investment. It is your first opportunity to get your foot in the door, so you want it to look right.

Resumes should give a complete, accurate picture of your background. Don't leave out positions or start your job history mid-career. Candidates often think that work experience outside their current field of employment or significant volunteer experience is unimportant or unnecessary information. In fact, such experiences may be important in certain situations. Someone in IT who spent three years as a paramedic may qualify for a clinically-oriented applications position that he or she would not have been considered for if that information was not included on his or her resume.

If you have been laid off, try not to panic. Do not write your resume immediately after the layoff because you may be feeling too negative about yourself. Wait until the dust settles and you have calmed down.

THE IMPORTANCE OF BEING VISIBLE

Marketing yourself goes well beyond your resume. A good marketer knows that being visible, building relationships, doing favors or good deeds, writing articles, speaking and volunteering are all important components of marketing.

Many of us assume that if we keep our heads down and do a good job, we will be rewarded. How many times have we heard that there's no time to get involved in outside organizations because there's too much to be done internally?

The truth is, such assumptions are wrong. Visibility both within your own organization and outside is extremely important to building a successful career.

Internally, it is important to document and get the word out when you've completed a major assignment, saved your organization a lot of money, implemented a new system that makes life easier, or achieved similar success. Don't be overly modest. Promoting yourself can be done in subtle, yet effective ways.

It's also important to get involved in non IT related projects. This gives you visibility in the organization as a contributing participant and not just as someone from IT.

There are many local and national organizations, such as healthcare associations and user groups, which will offer you increased visibility externally. Volunteering for committees, running for office and speaking at conferences give you broader visibility and credibility.

These activities not only expand your network of associates, but also make you more visible (and potentially viable) to recruiters and employers. The majority of good healthcare IT positions come from referrals through an individual's network of associates and the efforts of recruiters, who also depend upon networking, referrals, and cold calling from lists of conference attendees, speakers and authors.

There are many healthcare IT publications that accept articles from independent authors. If you've accomplished something outstanding or have a great idea, contact the editors of the appropriate publications to see if they will publish your article. When publications don't accept outside authors, you can still propose a concept and they may respond favorably.

This type of exposure can do wonders for a career. Many years ago, we were able to place a CIO who had no undergraduate degree with a very prestigious academic organization that required a master's degree. How did that happen? Because the individual was pictured on the cover of a publication, featured in an extensive article and named one of the top CIOs in the country. Obviously, the individual won the position through interviews, but the opportunity to interview was attributable to the credibility and exposure the candidate gained, in part, from the publication.

It's important to note that credibility should not be confused with showing off or being vain. It's good public relations and marketing. We do not advocate that you spend all of your time writing, speaking and serving on committees, but we do believe that maintaining a reasonable level of visibility and expanding your industry network is essential to marketing yourself.

GETTING INVOLVED

By getting involved in associations and interest groups, you create opportunities to build new relationships and gain credibility with a broader audience. Volunteering for committees and contributing your time and ideas builds credibility and trust. Speaking and writing on topics related to your specific knowledge and expertise also help you to market yourself.

As more people get to know you, recognize your unique skills and knowledge and appreciate your value, your realm of future job possibilities increases dramatically. If based on such exposure, people perceive that you are smart, well-informed and personable, you will be rewarded with referrals and possible job offers.

An important part of any marketing effort includes ongoing contact and follow-through on commitments.

When networking and building relationships, responding to ads, or meeting with recruiters—combined with your resume—gets you an interview, remember that you must continue to market yourself by making sure the interviewer understands your background, accomplishments and motivation. Dressing professionally, looking interviewers in the eye and exhibiting energetic body language are also part of marketing. We will discuss more about your approach to interviewing in Chapter 11.

Thank-you notes and appropriate, timely follow-up are equally important.

Even if you don't receive an offer of employment, or in the event that you reject an offer, the interview process should have been an outstanding marketing opportunity. Be appreciative. Let interviewers know how much you enjoyed talking with them and leave the door open for the future. A perfect position may develop in the future, or your interviewers may refer you for other opportunities.

Turning Plans into Action: Searching for New Opportunities

The quest for growth and challenge is the number one factor that drives people to seek new opportunities. As you evaluate a new position in healthcare IT, it is critical to analyze the job description and responsibilities to make sure that they are a departure from your current role and that you will be learning new skills that will further your career and development.

Healthcare organizations often hire people for their current skills, especially in the clinical and technical areas, because they desperately need to fill openings, and they show little concern for new employee growth and career paths. Indeed, the hiring person sometimes believes that if a new candidate is offered lots of money, he or she will forgo growth and challenge. Our advice in this regard is simple: do not follow a path that ignores growth and challenge. Figure 10-1, taken from the HIMSS / Hersher 2002 Job Satisfaction Survey, identifies some of the main reasons IT professionals leave their jobs to explore new opportunities.

FINDING THE RIGHT OPPORTUNITY

If you are looking for a new job because of a bad situation in your current environment, make sure the same conditions are not present in the new healthcare organization. That is not to say that a new environment will not be without its own challenges, but keep in mind that challenges offer opportunities for you to do exceptional things.

Changing jobs to pursue a new lifestyle has become totally acceptable and understandable to most new employers. For example, today's healthcare organizations respect individuals who change jobs to be closer to aging parents or to grandchildren, as long as the job fits the individual's goals for growth and challenge. However, if your new job fails to meet such goals, you will have wasted your time and a precious learning opportunity.

Set your priorities and systematically look for opportunities that fit them. At the same time, don't forget serendipity—the job that comes up out of the blue and looks too good to be true. It just may be the one. Only you can make that determination.

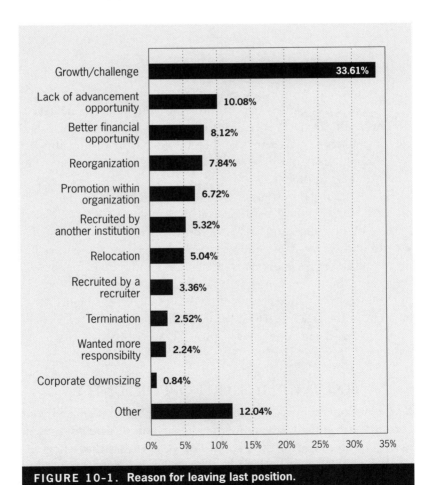

FIGURE 10-1. Reason for leaving last position.

Source: HIMSS/Hersher 2002 Job Satisfaction Survey.

DO YOUR HOMEWORK

When you face an opportunity to move to another position in healthcare IT, you must closely examine many factors. First and foremost, take a close look at the position itself. Will it offer an environment in which you can enhance your skills or learn new skills? Will you be exposed to newer technology? Is there a defined career path for continued growth with the new organization? These questions must be answered to your satisfaction before you go any further.

Do not invest your time or that of others, such as recruiters or human resources people, if the position doesn't fit your plan or requires a relocation that is impossible for you. If you need additional information to evaluate the opportunity, explain your issues and ask questions.

If the opportunity seems right on the surface and you decide to invest the time and energy to pursue it, there are many things that you must tackle. Evaluate and investigate the healthcare organization itself. Check out their Web site. Its reputation and financial state must be considered. Review every piece of information available to you and network with colleagues in the industry to find out what they know about the organization. Ask to see a financial or annual report. Bond documents are also a good tool to evaluate financial viability. *U.S. News and World Report* does annual reports on the nation's best hospitals, and other resources are available on the Internet.

Once you have established a good understanding of the type of organization it is, look closer. Review organizational charts. What is the reporting structure? Who will be your boss? Is there opportunity for growth and advancement? Is adequate funding available to accomplish the goals? What happened to your predecessor? Why did he or she leave? Where did he or she go?

Look for red flags and when you see them, address them. Don't wait. Once you've started a new position, it is too late to probe—you're already committed.

Another important factor is determining whether you fit the corporate culture. How well you fit the corporate culture will play a critical role during personal interviews. Ascertaining the fit can be a tough call, but your best bet is to ask yourself some basic questions and be honest with your answers. Do you like the people? Can you identify with and support the organization's missions and goals? Do you share the same work ethic? What is the physical environment like? Is the atmosphere formal or informal? Is it a verbal organization? What is the dress code? Do people socialize outside of work?

Do not take fitting the corporate culture lightly. You will be working, creating, problem solving, and, quite frankly, spending more than one-third of your life with your team. You'd better make sure you're on the same page and share common goals and values. If you do not fit the culture, you will probably not be happy and may find it hard to succeed.

HOW TO FIND THE RIGHT POSITION

There are many ways to find the right position in healthcare IT. When possible, use them all. Recruiters, ads, networking, internal promotions and the Internet are valuable sources for potential new jobs.

It has been our experience that the majority of people who changed jobs found their new jobs through recruiters or personal contacts. There are many ways to secure the job you want. Cover your bases when you are in an active job search and handle each approach thoroughly. Active job seekers should respond to ads.

Recruiting Firms. Working with recruiters can be a very effective way to secure your next position. There are two types of recruiters and recruitment firms: retained and contingency. It is important to understand the basic differences.

Retained recruiters are consultants who work exclusively on the searches they conduct. They should know the client organization very well and should get to know you well in the course of a search. They should provide you with information about the client, such as job descriptions and literature.

Retained firms are paid retainers by the clients, not the candidates, and work exclusively on the search. Retained search firms typically require in-person interviews prior to presenting candidates to their clients. If you are presented for interview with a client, you are probably one of three to six candidates the client will see. Most retained searches take from two to six months, so depending on when you are contacted in the process, do not be surprised if some time lapses before you go for a personal interview. Retained recruiters should keep you in the loop and share feedback with you as appropriate.

Contingency search firms and recruiters may or may not have an exclusive assignment to conduct searches. They are paid after they place a candidate. You need to ask contingency recruiters what their role is and what you can expect. Normally, you will not meet a contingency recruiter prior to an interview. Often contingency recruiters will not tell you the name of the organization until after they have presented your resume to the client. If you are concerned about confidentiality, this can present some of the same complications as a blind ad. You may want to ask contingency recruiters not to share your resume without your permission.

Regardless of whether you work with retained or contingency recruiters, be receptive and try to build relationships that can last throughout your career. If given the opportunity, share your long-term career goals and things that are important to you, such as family issues and location preferences. If you establish a positive relationship, the same recruiter or firm may work with you for many years to help you accomplish your goals. As with anything in life, it pays to be nice, helpful and to listen. If you are not interested in a position you may be a referral source. Referrals are the best way to identify candidates.

Ads. Ads appear in many different publications and Web sites so take the time to review several. If you cannot move, review all local publications and Web sites and scan national journals for positions in your area. Remember that some companies only post positions on their own Web sites.

When you respond to ads, be sure to pay particular attention to your cover letter. Make it direct and to the point. Proof it carefully, as misspellings and grammatical errors can lead to you being rejected before your resume is thoroughly reviewed. In your cover letter, call attention to important points and, if necessary, expand on key information in your resume. It is a good idea to follow up by phone to see if your response has been received.

Be careful about responding to blind ads if you don't want others to know that you are looking for a new job. You can never be certain who ran a blind ad and who may see your resume.

Networking. Even though we have a multitude of online job markets and newspaper ads, 60 to 70 percent of the best jobs are hidden, and we have no way of knowing about them through the media. So how do you find that new and exciting job you have always wanted? Networking is the answer. Someone may know someone who has a job for you.

There are three types of networking. The first involves working with someone with whom you have a very secure relationship. When you first begin networking, you may still be slightly unclear about your skills. An ideal way to identify your special attributes is to sit down with a known coach or mentor, lay your cards on the table, and say, "I'd like to bounce some ideas off of you about my career growth. Are they realistic? Are they attainable? What are your ideas about my skills? Can you help me refocus my thoughts?" For this kind of networking to be effective, you and the other person must know each other extremely well.

The second kind of networking can be both the most difficult and the most successful. It involves meeting or talking with a person you have identified as a networking resource. The person could be the author of an article that interests you, a member of an organization you belong to, an industry expert you have always admired or a peer on a national level that you respect. As networking is a difficult task, particularly with people you do not know, you need to be very upbeat in your approach.

People's time is extremely valuable. Therefore, when you ask someone for help, you need to be well prepared. For example, you should know what kinds of positions you are interested in and have appropriate questions ready to ask. You may have from 5 to 20 network contacts in this category, so approach them all. If you approach your networking in an honest, direct manner, you will find that about 1 out of 10 contacts will bring you some value. That value could be a referral to another individual, some ideas about education and skills you may want to acquire or a potential new job.

The results are not always immediate. If you have had a good informational interview, your contact will want to spend some time thinking about jobs and individuals he or she can connect you with. The opportunity could arise even three months later, when your networking resource is having dinner with a colleague and that person mentions a job opening that would be perfect for you. When you are networking, especially with this particular group, you will get more information from face-to-face or phone conversations than you will from e-mail or "snail mail."

The third type of networking, which is also very valuable, is expressing your interests in new career opportunities to your peers, your family, your friends, members of social and charitable organizations you belong to, and so on. You never know when an acquaintance may have excellent connections for helping in your quest for career growth.

Remember:
- Networking means you are taking someone's time, so use that time wisely.
- Networking means that you follow up with every single contact and thank him or her.
- Networking means that from time to time you check in, either by phone, in person or by e-mail, to let your contacts know of your status.

The single most important thing to remember about networking is that people will not take the time to see you or evaluate you unless they are interested in you. If you can keep in mind that you have something valuable to offer, each meeting will be worthwhile for both parties. Networkers will work with you, even if they do not know you, because at one point or another in their careers, they networked. So when it's your turn and you have the opportunity to answer someone's query for more information, remember that you owe someone who helped you in the past.

Networking is an absolute must in a job search. Talking with your contacts about your goals and current job situation is probably the best method, along with professional recruiters, to secure the right position. If people know what you are looking for, they will call you when they hear of something appropriate.

Networking in an Academic Healthcare Environment. Networking in an academic environment such as an academic medical center (AMC) is extremely commonplace. However, if you are trying to conduct a quiet search or a harmless inquiry, be cautious. Gossip runs rampant. The same holds true for soliciting references. One department chair will think nothing of calling a peer to check out a potential candidate. Academic references are extensive and can be very easy to access. If you are in serious discussions with an AMC, ask them to maintain your confidentiality. However, a wide circle of references at an AMC can be beneficial for candidates, as they have many opportunities to check out a potential employer.

THE IMPORTANCE OF FLEXIBILITY

The market will always fluctuate. Corporate cultures are becoming more diverse every day, and required skills are changing just as rapidly. All of these factors make it difficult for job seekers to interpret their fit within a job, a corporate climate and a healthcare organization's long-term goals. Accordingly, in such an environment, one of your greatest personal attributes could very well be your flexibility.

Flexibility in dealing with a moving target is a positive trait somewhat like patience. You may not identify flexibility as a valued strength. When you conduct self-assessments, you think specifically of your experience or accomplishments with IT, finance, clinical skills management and so on. Realistically, we all have qualifications—the special or unique abilities and accomplishments that we have to offer potential employers. Being skilled, however, is not the only qualification. More than likely, there will be numerous other job seekers with the same skill level as you. Others may have equal or greater experience than you.

So how can you stand apart?

Today, employers look not only at your skill level but also at your personal style. When a potential employer reviews your resume, terms such as "team player" and "project management" often stand out. Your personal style is very important, and flexibility could be the differentiator in your job search.

Flexibility can have many meanings. As a professional, you will need to be flexible in terms of what you can do, how much you know, and what you are willing to learn. Gone are the days of the specialist and the one-dimensional professional. Enter the multi-experienced multi-tasker with multiple skills. The actual "specialist" or analyst in healthcare may have to hold back some excellent talent and delay some projects. Do we really need a pharmacist to install a new pharmacy system? No, not really. The log jam is finally breaking up. Proven project managers are being accepted regardless of their specialties.

When you are seeking the right opportunity, however, flexibility can have an entirely different meaning. Your ability to be flexible will greatly depend upon your needs and goals. For example, if your goal is to do Job X and you don't receive an offer, do you have the experience or skills to do Job Y? If you do not land the job you wanted, but the organization likes you enough to hire you, you should consider the opportunity valuable because of the experience and skills you will gain.

You may also need to be flexible about salary. For instance, if you seek X amount of dollars, can you still meet your needs if you receive slightly less and other elements of the position are excellent? Think about your ideal working environment and the specific opportunities that would match your needs. The job you accept may not be your perfect job, but if you are flexible, it may ultimately help you achieve your goals.

These issues underscore the importance of doing a thorough self-assessment before you begin your job search. A self-assessment will enable you to analyze your skills and personal style and, ultimately, determine your flexibility. Chances are that you will not get the exact job you're looking for. So figure out how flexible you're willing to be.

DEALING WITH REJECTION

When you begin looking for new opportunities, be prepared to deal with the ups and downs. Rejection can be difficult to handle. Unfortunately, the hard truth is that most candidates do not get the first job they interview for, or even the third or fourth. Many times the most perfectly qualified candidate does not get the job. You must always remember that rejection is not personal.

There are many reasons for being rejected. Sometimes it is logical and sometimes it isn't. The employer's interview schedule or failure to interview well may have favored another candidate. Perhaps the interviewer didn't understand or really read your resume. Frequently, an interviewer has spoken with several well-qualified candidates besides you and had better chemistry with someone else. The most common reasons for not hiring a candidate are that it wasn't the right fit, time or place; the position was put on hold; or the position was filled by someone with internal connections.

Even if you think you are prepared for rejection, when you are focused on finding a new opportunity, every disappointment feels like a blow. Keep moving ahead with confidence. Odds are that it wasn't the right fit for you anyway. A perfect match is out there somewhere.

Dealing with rejection takes a lot of strength, introspection and knowledge about who you are and what you're capable of handling. Remain confident and try to find out why you were rejected. It is important to keep moving forward and try to learn from the experience.

Be sure to thank the potential employer for the opportunity and mention your interest in being considered in the future if something appropriate develops. Be comfortable asking what you might have done differently and what skills you were lacking. If you harbor resentment, you may project negativity or insecurity, which will increase the likelihood of you being rejected on your next interview.

Draw on your inner strength. Present a positive, enthusiastic attitude, a good sense of humor and an eagerness to move into a new role. Potential employers want to hire employees who are positive and want the position.

Once you find that great new job, you will forge a partnership with your new employer. As is the case in all partnerships, you must be willing and able to compromise from time to time. It's important to reach a good balance. Clearly, you can't afford to be overly stubborn, but it's also detrimental to be too compromising. Based on your own comfort level, you should be aware of what seems right to you. It is important to note that although compromise is mutual between an employer and an employee, a corporate culture may not change to meet your needs. Even if you are a valued employee, you are still only one part of the organizational whole.

Keep in mind that throughout your professional career, you will always be asked to adapt to new ideas and new environments. Business means progress. Progress means change. Change requires adaptability. Adaptability requires flexibility. And the more capable you are in this regard, the easier it will be for you to make transitions over the course of your career. Your career will never grow stagnant as long as you remain flexible.

CHAPTER 11

The Interview Process

Congratulations! You've marketed yourself well and secured an interview with a potential employer, who was most likely impressed with the credentials you presented on your resume. That should give you a certain degree of confidence you can use to your advantage when you interview. Remember, though, that the level of self-marketing increases during an interview. This is your opportunity to present yourself in person as opposed to on paper.

Interviewing is a two-way street. The interviewer will ask you questions and you must be prepared to ask questions of the interviewer. Not every interviewer knows how to interview. Interviewing is an art and takes practice and skill.

Just because an interviewer has your resume, you can't assume your resume has been carefully reviewed. Make sure that you are able to discuss your background and accomplishments. Everything you do and say during an interview is evaluated, even if it is not part of a formal question or discussion. Even questions about what you enjoy doing in your spare time or what hobbies you enjoy may be part of your evaluation.

Nothing during a job search is more nerve-racking than preparing and living through the first interview. The first hurdle to pass is to make sure that you are seriously considering leaving your current job, even if it is for an internal transfer. Nothing cools an interviewer faster than an applicant who says, "I'm not sure that I'm ready to make a job change." What a waste of everyone's time!

The first impression you make is the most important. Read a reputable "How to Get a Job" book for details. Boiled down to one sentence, the advice is: look and feel good and if that means buying a new suit, go for it. Interviewing is like dating; you need to feel good about yourself and the person you are meeting.

A professional appearance is critical and sets the initial reaction in an interview. Although we would all like to think that our skills and accomplishments stand alone, the truth is that people judge us by their first impression, so that impression must be positive, not negative. When in doubt, be conservative and understated.

You have to prepare for the interview. It is perfectly acceptable to ask for a copy of the job description and information about the organization prior to your interview. You should also visit the organization's Web site, where you can usually find helpful information. Find out as much as you can about the people you are meeting, including their titles, the correct spellings of their names and their backgrounds. Review the job description, then relax and get a good night's sleep. Remember you have something important to offer—otherwise a busy manager wouldn't take the time to see you.

At all times, use your instincts—trust them and act on them. It is always useful to arrive a few minutes early and observe. You can learn a lot about the organization's friendliness, pace and dress code by observing and paying attention to how you are treated. Watch for these subtle clues because title and salary are only part of the total picture. If you are not comfortable in the environment, it is probably not the right place for you. The culture, the team, your boss, the job content, and your future growth potential are key factors in determining your continued interest in the position.

When you interview, always focus on being positive, attentive and enthusiastic. Make direct eye contact, listen and smile. Be sure to project an energetic style. That does not mean that you should sell yourself too hard. Pushing too hard to convince interviewers that you are qualified can backfire, particularly if you lack specific experience that they consider critical.

Try to make a personal connection during the interview. For example, discuss similar alma maters, hometowns or hobbies with your interviewers. That is not to say you should wonder far off topic, but a personal connection can influence the outcome of an interview. You need to like the people you work with. That first meeting is a skills qualifier and a chance to get to know you. While you are interviewing, make sure that you really understand the position and the organizational structure.

OUTCOMES NEEDED AFTER FIRST INTERVIEW

- What are the expectations for the position?
- What resources are available?
- Are the deadlines realistic?
- Are you comfortable being yourself?
- Does your interviewer show you the environment?
- Are you introduced to coworkers?
- Does the interviewer show an interest in you as a balanced person and not just a commodity?
- Is the interviewer comfortable when you ask questions?

Using personal examples is always an effective method of answering questions. Be yourself and get to know the people interviewing you. Ask your own questions. Prepare a list of information that you want to discuss in the first meeting. Jotting questions on a notepad to take with you would be valuable, so that you can remember the things you want answered before you leave. Taking notes is more than acceptable. This is an opportunity to appear informed and interested. Remember, interviews are two-way streets.

QUESTIONS TO ASK YOUR POTENTIAL BOSS

- What is the organization's financial picture?
- How stable is the senior management team?
- How has the organization been impacted by outside forces?
- What is the managed care penetration, and how is the organization dealing with it?
- Does your boss understand the implications of HIPAA?
- Have there been any talks about mergers, alliances, or takeovers?
- Is IT ready for e-healthcare, and who is pushing it on the executive team?
- And finally, and most difficult of all, what are your potential boss's career aspirations, and will he or she be around to mentor you?

For some, interviewing is a real challenge. For others, it's downright terrifying. Even the most confident individuals can find interviewing nerve-wracking. If the truth be known, the interview actually starts well before your appointed meeting time.

You should be relaxed but very professional before, during, and after an interview because everything you do around the interview is, in actuality, part of the interview. The minute you walk in the door, you are being evaluated. How did you treat the receptionist? How did you respond to directions? Did you live up to your resume? You should pay attention to every detail as you go through the interview process.

When the interview is over, be sure to ask for the interviewer's business card so that you can correctly spell his or her name in the follow-up thank-you letter you will write. In fact, an extremely smart thing to do is to hand the administrative assistant your card as you leave so that it can be on file for future reference.

Interviewing is not about rehashing your skills and accomplishments. Instead, it is about getting to know the person you will be working with. It is also about verifying first impressions, discovering information about the position, corporate culture, and organization, and, ultimately, determining whether this is the right position for you.

FOLLOW-UP INTERVIEWS

If you are interviewing for a managerial position, you can assume that there will be two interviews. The first interview is focused on getting acquainted, determining compatibility and assessing the desirability of working for that particular organization.

The second interview is typically with a larger group of people and involves asking and answering many hard questions. Salary questions are rarely asked in the first interview, nor is there usually a detailed discussion about benefits.

It is important to recognize that not everyone is a good interviewer. Try to interpret each interviewer appropriately and don't rush to conclusions. A bad interviewer does not make a bad boss. Not all interviewers realize their weaknesses, so you may need to help them out.

Frequently, group interviews are part of an interview schedule. Connect with each member of the group, understand his or her position with the organization and learn a little bit about his or her background. Be sure to look at everyone during the interview, even though it's important to focus on the individual asking the questions. Try to keep group interviews interactive. Don't be intimidated. Ask your questions. It's often very interesting to get the group members' perspectives on a variety of issues.

During a second or third interview, you may be asked to present to a group. This can be an excellent opportunity to show your presentation skills and to observe the group dynamics that you will be working with if you accept the position. This will tell you a lot about the corporate culture. Presentations need not be terribly formal. Use the style that you are most comfortable with, whether that includes a PowerPoint presentation, flip charts or a presentation without visual aids. Your content, communication style, interaction with the group and ability to field questions are most important.

Ask everyone you interview with what the corporate culture is like. A good question to ask your potential boss is what in your background caught his or her interest. A very telling clue about the culture is whether your interviewer asks you anything about yourself. It is important for your boss to have an impression of who you are as a human being because you'll be spending many hours a day interacting.

The key questions that need to be answered to your satisfaction are:
- What is it like to work here?
- What is the corporate culture like?
- Are employees promoted from within?
- Do employees ever get together socially?
- What's expected of employees?
- What's the work ethic here?

After the second interview, your intuition plus your evaluation of the job potential will help you draw some firm conclusions. Do your potential peers appear satisfied? Do they speak with respect about their boss and the organization? Do you respect the goals of the department and the strategic direction of the overall enterprise, and do they meet your values?

Of course, there are other factors to interviewing that you need to avoid. Don't be late to interviews and try to avoid excuses. Don't divulge too much detail or go on and on, never allowing the interviewer to talk. Don't ask about trivial details, such as how much does parking cost or how much time is allowed for lunch. These types of questions are not appropriate during the interview process and may give the impression that you are more interested in the little details than the job and the organization. Focus your questions and answers at the right level.

In general, interviews should be thought of as opportunities. Your qualifications got you in the door, and you clearly have a lot to offer. Make the most of your opportunity and market yourself appropriately.

CHAPTER 12

Assessing the Corporate Culture

No matter how great a potential new job sounds, how do you determine whether it's the right corporate culture for you? Next to a position being a good move and offering a strong opportunity for growth, corporate culture is the most important success factor for any potential candidate.

As defined by the Harvard Business Review, "Culture is what remains to bolster a company's identity as one organization. Without culture a company lacks values, direction and purpose." A large part of making the right career moves involves understanding one's own personal and professional needs and determining whether an organization's corporate culture meets those needs.

One of your goals in evaluating not only corporate culture but also IT culture should be to ascertain that the organization will enable you to achieve your professional goals and to reach self-actualization, the highest level of Maslow's Hierarchy of Human Needs, as illustrated in Figure 12-1.

Organizations are becoming increasingly aware of and sensitive to their employees as well-balanced individuals, and it is management's responsibility to provide a supportive work environment that allows people to grow professionally and feel good about their contributions. As you seriously consider a job, the key factors to assess are the culture, the team, your prospective boss, the position's content and the future growth potential. Last but not least is whether the position fits your lifestyle. Is it in a location where you and your family or significant other can be very happy? Only you can judge if the job itself and its content will offer you growth. Only you and your family can judge whether location and lifestyle are what you're looking for.

Ultimately, you'll have to use your intuition to evaluate the corporate culture over the course of a series of interviews.

DO YOU FIT THE CORPORATE CULTURE?

- Can you identify with and support the organization's mission and goals?
- Do you like the people?
- Do you share the same work ethic?
- Is the environment formal or informal?
- Do the members of the organization communicate and share?

The cultural match will make a successful and happy long-term employee. It's a two-way relationship: The employee must match the culture, and the culture must match the employee and his or her growth needs and comfort level. Your evaluation of an organization's

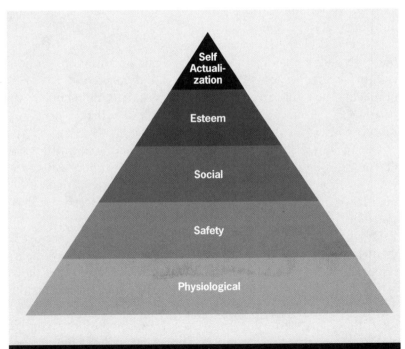

FIGURE 12-1. Maslow's Hierarchy of Human Needs.

culture should start from the very first phone call. How you are treated from day one clearly indicates how you'll be treated throughout your career in the organization.

There are many ways to look at an organization. Some are qualitative, some are quantitative and some are intuitive. For now, let's look at the intuitive ways.

Before your interview, do as much research as you can on the Internet. If the company is publicly traded, you should be able to find an annual report. Also visit the organization's Web site. From a Web site and company publications, you can tell a lot about how an organization feels about its employees, customers and role in the community.

As you go through your various interviews, it is important to observe the organization and be prepared to ask questions that may seem slightly unusual and not related to job content. For example:

- Can you tell me what the corporate culture is like?
- Is this a verbal organization?
- Is this an organization that works through memos and e-mails?
- Is this an organization that uses the Internet only?
- How are decisions made?
- How are decisions shared or communicated?
- What part will I have in the senior decision-making body?

As you are interviewing or negotiating, watch for answers to the following questions:

- How do the members of this organization negotiate?
- Are they fair, caring and honest?
- Do they like each other?

As you are evaluating a culture, you need to decide whether you will like your potential coworkers, the people you are going to be with eight to twelve hours a day. And most important, can you learn from them? Do you respect them? Is it a team environment, and, if so, how will you fit into the team? And most importantly, can you learn from them? A very good question to ask during the interview process might be, "How does a newcomer become a member of the team?" A question to ask your potential peers is how mistakes are treated.

Think once again of interviewing as similar to dating. On the first date, you ask yourself if you like the people, if you like the environment, and if you would like to come back for a second date. Then, on your second date, you start asking some really hard, primarily business-related questions. You can often tell by the way people answer your questions what kind of an environment you might potentially be working in.

It is critical that you ask what expectations the organization has for the job and what support you will be given to get the job done. If your interviewers object to such questions, and if the answers to such questions are important to you, the organization will not be a good fit for you.

By evaluating the answers to questions asked during interviews, garnering opinions from current and former employers and gauging the general reputation of the organization in the marketplace, a candidate can determine whether an organization has the type of corporate culture that fits his or her needs.

On your third set of interviews, which should be your final set of interviews, it is really important to bring your spouse or partner to help you evaluate the environment. Who knows you best but the people that you live with? It would be wise on your final interview cycle to do what we call "break bread." No, we're not interested in whether people eat sloppily or spill soup on their clothes. We're interested in how they act and how they treat you in a social situation.

If at any time during the interview process something doesn't feel right, you need to go back and check it out. We now move from the dating metaphor to the marriage metaphor. How many of us have dated or married people that we were sure would change once we were married? People don't change, and environments don't change easily. As a result, that cultural match is very important for you and for the people hiring you.

As we've looked around the country in the last couple of years, we've seen a very interesting change. That change reflects back to about 30 years ago, when people really looked to their work environment as a second home. Today, people want to be in an environment where they can grow, produce, and earn respect, while knowing that people feel good about them. They also want to know that they are in an environment where people can critique each other's behavior and work and still walk out the door at the end of a meeting as friends, or at least as good business colleagues.

As we mentioned earlier, more and more people are considering relocation and lifestyle issues as they look to change jobs. To move your family across the country for your new position only to find out you don't fit in the corporate environment becomes a disaster.

When we are looking at what we call replacement positions, we typically ask the hiring manager why the person left. Often the answer is that the person didn't fit in. Who was responsible for that? Obviously, both sides were culpable. The hiring manager wanted the person to fit in, and the person who took the job wanted to fit in, but it still didn't work out. It is imperative that you walk away from a situation that looks as if it isn't going to work for you.

Are truly great corporate cultures difficult to find? The answer is yes. To make a good choice, you need to evaluate who you are as an individual and what is important to you. Benefits make up a very interesting portion of the package. Because many of us must cope with aging parents, small children or partners with special needs, we need a work environment that is reasonably forgiving and understanding of the many factors we must balance in our lives. That balance is key if we are to perform as outstanding employees.

As you are evaluating a corporate culture, you need to look not only at your bosses and your peers, but also at your key users. How will you be able to work with them? What are their expectations? How will they respond to you? And how will you respond to them? Do you really understand what their needs are? Can you teach them, work with them and help them to set priorities and understand your priorities for projects?

Currently the healthcare job market is stronger than most other sectors. There has been enough turmoil in healthcare to last us a lifetime, and there is a great deal of turmoil coming. It is extremely important that you not jump at the first job you interview for if something in the back of your mind tells you that you don't belong there. On the other hand, if you walk into an environment and immediately say, "I love it! This is the place for me!" take a step back, go through the second and third interviews, and verify your initial impressions.

Your potential new employer will check your references. There is nothing wrong with checking your new employer's references as well. Talk to former employees to find out what the environment is truly like. The openness of the interview process will tell you a great deal about your new potential environment. Will you be given access to all the people you'd like to meet? Does your job call for you to meet board members? Will you be allowed to meet with them privately? Will you be able to ask them tough questions? What threats does the organization face? How can you help? What does the organization need to do in the next two years? Who are their competitors? Do they have any merger talks? If so, where would you fit?

If you are satisfied that the job is right for you, move into the negotiating phase. If you are being hired at a high enough level, it is important to consider the need for an employment contract. Cultures can change with new CEOs. If your bosses start changing, if the organization enters into a merger or if the board suddenly puts a clamp on all of your new projects, you need to have an out. That out is an employee contract. Sometimes these conditions exist as you consider a new position, making the need for a contract even more critical.

An employee contract needs to be carefully negotiated because many such contracts define the employer's expectations of the employee. If the expectations in your contract are reasonable and the support you will receive is reasonable, you have made a good match. If the expectations are unreasonable and there's no support, it will be impossible for you to perform your job. You will need both flexibility and creativity to negotiate the best possible contract for you. Understand that many organizations will only offer contracts at the most senior levels. Others will not agree to contracts at any level, but it never hurts to try and negotiate.

We also want to be able to make a difference in the organization we work for. These factors play into evaluating the culture of any organization you're seriously considering as the next step in your career growth.

Finally, you need to evaluate the corporate culture in terms of your continuing career growth. Will the new cultural environment pigeonhole you in one job and deny you the opportunity to grow? Remember, we've seen a sudden shift. More and more people would like to stay in an organization and grow into other responsibilities. Will the new organization allow you to do that? Or in five years will you be faced with the need to relocate yourself and your family to yet another job and yet another situation where you will be pigeonholed in a job without growth? Think about it. Your choice has far-reaching implications, and most of them are dictated by the corporate culture.

CHAPTER 13

Relocation

Because healthcare is one of the strongest industries today and because IT professionals seem to be in neverending demand, job opportunities present themselves throughout the nation and even the world. We are seeing evidence of this for all positions, from CIOs to project leaders to programmers. National or international demand can greatly increase the scope and potential promise of your job search. Clearly, it offers a strong motivation to leave your home and your family roots, because many of the best jobs will necessitate relocation. But it can also have daunting implications for someone who has grown up in one location and has spent a majority of his or her life there.

Relocation is a major issue, not only for a job candidate, but also for the candidate's family, extended family and friends. A potential relocation should not be taken lightly. Let's say that a candidate says moving to a new location is no problem. In further discussions, however, it may come to light that he or she has a junior in high school, a senior in high school and aging parents. This must be treated seriously.

Think through the reality of a move before you consider interviewing for a new position. It is costly and time consuming for an employer to interview candidates that require relocation. Don't lead an employer into thinking that you can relocate when in actuality you have not even discussed the possibility with your family or support system.

Never assume that your family will happily go wherever the best opportunity for you happens to be located. Often, a spouse or significant other will appear to be supportive until the discussions with a potential employer become serious; then their true feelings come pouring out. If you are settled in a secure position, you may feel less interested in relocation, even for a fabulous position. Unfortunately, there are times when unemployment as a result of a downsizing, merger, bankruptcy or just plain firing forces the issue.

If you are unemployed and relocation seems necessary to secure an appropriate position, you must still go through the same evaluation process. If your family will be miserable or if you don't have the support necessary for the move to be successful, you may need to reevaluate your priorities and either consider positions that will require you to travel without relocating or expand the range of positions you are willing to consider.

If you are interested in a position outside your local area, it is advisable to discuss it with your family as soon as possible. During the discussion, make sure that everyone understands that you need to know exactly what his or her thoughts and concerns are about a move. Relocating is not an easy process. Often at least one child objects to moving. There may be aging parents or custody issues to consider. If the job of your dreams comes along and you have a child who is a senior in high school, what do you do? If your spouse or partner is in the middle of a major project at work and cannot leave for a significant period of time, what do you do?

Many families figure out a compromise or opt to pass on a job. Once you get all the details ironed out, you can go into the interview process with a clear head, knowing that you have the support of those around you. You can then seriously consider if the opportunity is right for you.

Assuming that the job looks great, the location is wonderful and your family and friends are supportive, what do you look for next? At this point, it is critical to examine all the other elements of the environment that are important to you: schools, leisure activities, climate, community structure and opportunities for employment and career advancement for your spouse or partner. Make sure that on your second or third interview you are able to bring your family with you and have the time to show them the locale and seek out an optimal neighborhood in which to live.

Make sure to evaluate the new area carefully. It must fit the entire family. Compare the new cost of living with your current cost of living. Look closely at real estate, school districts, recreational opportunities and cultural amenities. If the public schools are marginal, your children may need to attend private schools, which will need to be taken into account as you negotiate your new salary. The job might look perfect on the surface, but if it is located in an area that does not meet your needs and your family's needs, it is not the right opportunity for you.

Jumping to another job without considering the total picture can be a mistake and may cause a career setback. Be sure to look at the things that are important to everyone in your family. Your prospective employer should be able to help you find the information you need or point you in the right direction. The local Chamber of Commerce should also be able to provide a great deal of helpful information.

Several cost-of-living-comparison services are available on the Internet. You can also independently research Web sites for comparative cost-of-living information. Remember, such sites provide only averaged information. Costs may vary dramatically based on specific suburbs or neighborhoods. Among the Web sites that offer cost-of-living comparisons and related employment relocation information are:

www.homefair.com
www.virtualrelocation.com
www.datamasters.com

Local real estate agents should be able to provide the most accurate comparisons based on your needs. Finding a good real estate agent is important, particularly if you plan to buy a house or condominium. Your prospective employer should be able to help you make some connections. If that is not the case, ask a real estate agent in your hometown for recommendations and interview candidates by phone until you settle on someone you feel comfortable with. That person should send you information and listing sheets on properties that meet your requirements before you visit. Typically, when you visit for your second interview, that is a good time to meet with a real estate agent to look at the area and properties in your price range.

If you are seriously considering a job in an area with a much higher cost of living, you may have to consider purchasing a smaller property or renting for a period of time. This is also an important topic to discuss with family members early in the process. When hiring for a senior-level position, an employer may be willing to help offset the cost within an extremely expensive housing market. Your accountant should be engaged to help you review such issues.

Last, but not least, the relocation package is critical. Candidates often accept or reject jobs based on the generosity of the moving package. In most cases, a new employee should not be expected to bear the costs of moving. In fact, today's moving packages are often creative and may allow employers some leeway to compensate for set salary ranges. For example, some employers may be able to add a little extra money beyond the physical moving costs that you can use as you choose.

Most healthcare organizations do not pay closing points or real estate agents' fees. And unless you are being hired at a very senior executive level, most do not buy your home or help you meet two house payments until you sell your original home.

Among the costs that are frequently covered in a moving package are one or more house-hunting trips for you and your spouse or significant other, movement of your household goods (often based on the least expensive of three estimates), a few months of temporary housing (three to six months on average, with a limit on the monthly amount of rent) and, in some cases, flights back and forth to your city of origin until your family moves to the new location.

Some organizations own or lease corporate apartments to help new employees make the transition into the area. If temporary housing is not included in your package and you feel that you need it, ask; it may be a negotiable item.

If an organization's relocation policies are very structured and offer little room for negotiation, it may be able to offset the cost of your relocation by offering you a one-time signing bonus or putting you on salary a month early so that you can do a couple of consulting projects tied to your house-hunting visits. Before you accept a job in a new location, you should contact your accountant, because many issues related to moving packages may have unfavorable tax consequences. In some cases, an organization will adjust the amount you are given to offset the tax ramifications.

Even if everything checks out appropriately from a job standpoint, family standpoint and financial standpoint, double-check all the details before you pack up that moving van. The last thing you want to do is accept a job and three months later say, "Oops, I can't live here." Never forget that despite all the hard work it entails, relocating to a new city can be a great adventure and a very positive experience for you and your family.

CHAPTER 14

Offers and Negotiations

Y ou have made it through the interview process and are the candidate of choice. You will now begin the most delicate part of the entire process—evaluating and negotiating the offer. It remains a process that is very similar to dating. You've gone through the interview cycle, you've met all of the people (the whole family, including in-laws and cousins) and right now you like each other. The role they have chosen for you is one you feel you can do and certainly one through which you can advance. The corporate culture, just like a new family of your own choosing, is one that makes you comfortable. You believe in their values, mission and goals.

The decision to make the transition should be exciting and, in the long run, fun. Nonetheless, the challenge of changing jobs is hard work and not to be taken lightly. If at any point in the process your intuition says that you are heading in the wrong direction—stop.

People change jobs for many different reasons. Interestingly, money (as long as the amount is equitable and fair) is not first or second on the list. What motivates people to change jobs is growth or challenge and respect for their work. Location and lifestyle have increasingly become factors in the decision to move. That does not mean candidates are planning to work less but rather that they value balance in their lives. Being close to family or being in an area where the educational system and extracurricular activities support their children's needs has become a critical deciding factor for many people.

Corporate culture, mission and leadership are also becoming more important factors in job changes. They may indeed be the keys to securing desired job candidates. If new employees do not fit into the culture, they will find it difficult to advance, and advancement is what job applicants are seeking.

Your job needs to be clearly defined, with definite benchmarks for success. There should be a job description or position profile that outlines responsibilities and expectations. The organizational environment should support career growth, and you should be able to see many obvious examples of such growth. You need to like, respect and trust your boss and the executive team. If there are traits in your boss or issues in the corporate culture that you do not like, you are not going to be able to change them. Remember, a bad job decision, made for the wrong reasons, is not easily defendable on a resume.

If the interviewing process is going well and you have decided that you really want the job, you should think about all the factors that will determine whether you accept the offer, including salary, benefits, vacation time, work schedule, reporting relationship, travel requirements, start date and anything else that is important to you. Never negotiate for a position that you don't want. Nothing is more frustrating, and sometimes embarrassing, for a hiring manager than to work hard to meet a candidate's needs and demands and then have the candidate reject the offer.

TIPS FOR NEGOTIATING

Remember, honesty and directness are critical. We have seen candidates make ridiculous demands that they know an organization cannot possibly meet as a means of rejecting an offer that they never really wanted. This type of behavior makes the recruiter or human resources person responsible for screening look foolish or poorly informed and can anger the hiring manager. In a fairly close-knit industry like healthcare IT, such candidates should remember that they might well encounter the same people again when seeking another position that they truly want.

During negotiations, be careful that your demands do not cross the line. Explain your needs and requests clearly and reasonably. You will be working with these people, so it is important not to appear greedy, angry, confused, emotional or rigid during negotiations. If your basic needs cannot be met, you should close the discussions in a professional manner. Keep the door open for the future. You never know when paths may cross or a different, more appropriate opportunity may develop.

Once you receive an offer for a job that you are interested in taking, make sure that you fully understand the terms and have all of the information necessary to make an informed decision. It is always a good idea to leave the door wide open as you negotiate. Never make discussion-ending statements, such as "That is completely unacceptable." Rather, be positive and appreciative of the offer and tactfully state your concerns. Keep your requests realistic. No matter how much a company may want to hire you, if you respond inappropriately, negotiations may blow up.

Compromise and creativity are critical tools for a good negotiator. If you are really interested, constantly reassure the other party. Focus on the critical must-haves and let some of the not-so-critical issues go. Make suggestions. Don't assume that the person issuing the offer has thought of all the options. Remember that how a candidate negotiates and is recruited into an organization sets the tone for the rest of his or her term of employment.

An offer consists of many elements. It is not just a base salary and bonus. The ideal offer will define what the expectations of the position are and what support you will receive from senior management to do your job effectively. An offer should include a base, a bonus (if part of the package) and an explanation of how that bonus is achieved. It should identify all the perks and benefits that you are eligible for. In some organizations, the salary you are offered may be pushing the top of the scale. If you have decided you really want the position but the offer is not quite what you need, work with the hiring manager.

There are many different ways to get the money you need to accept the job of your dreams. For example, you may be able to negotiate a sign-on bonus. If the organization cannot give you the salary you need because it would lead to inequity with your new peers, you could ask the firm to do something creative, such as putting you on salary a month early. Or if you have always wanted to get a master's degree but have never had the money for it, you might ask if the organization has an educational reimbursement fund.

Negotiating is difficult because ultimately both sides must win. Therefore, if you try to over negotiate, the offer may be withdrawn.

Even if you get the job, if you were pushy and difficult to deal with during negotiations, people will remember that for a long time. Make the negotiations a pleasant process for everyone. Obviously, you don't want to give in if it will cost you a lot of money, but it is important to understand the situation from your employer's position.

If you are working with a recruiter, make sure to ask for advice. Negotiations are the hardest part of the job-hunting process, and the recruiter should be there to help you. Use all of the resources you have at hand, including your accountant, recruiter, family, friends and associates. Also make sure to get the phone numbers of some of your peers and your boss at your new job so you can call to ask questions. It helps to get all aspects of the offer ironed out before you receive the formal piece of paper. Once an offer is down on paper, it is fairly finalized.

Remember, just like in dating, people don't want to be rejected. Once an employer has given you an offer based on your negotiations, it is uncomfortable for both parties if you come back and say, "Oh, excuse me. I forgot to tell you that I am going to lose $10,000 in my pension fund and that I'd like you to make that up." Make sure you have covered all your bases before closing negotiations.

Negotiation is a process that doesn't happen overnight, so you should take the time to do it right. If you negotiate well, the people at your new job will be proud and eager to work with you, and, most important of all, they will realize that you are a team player who is anxious to support the organization.

No matter how well you negotiate, you may still need to say no to a job offer. After all, if you are truly committed to pursuing career growth, it would be a mistake to settle for a position that doesn't meet your expectations. If you cannot strike an appropriate accord with a potential employer, remain professional and simply say "No, thank you."

NEVER BURN YOUR BRIDGES

When you accept a new position, you face the difficult task of resigning from your current position. It is extremely important to handle the resignation professionally and respectfully so that as you move forward, you retain a positive relationship and good references. You never know when you may cross paths with people from your current workplace again.

A resignation should never be tendered by letter, e-mail or voice mail. You owe your boss a face-to-face meeting in which you explain why you are accepting a new position and express your appreciation for his or her support and the opportunities he or she has given you. Be sure to offer a reasonable transition period. Two weeks of notice is generally acceptable for lower-level positions, and four weeks of notice or more is common in more senior jobs.

If your organization extends a counteroffer, you should be prepared to reject it. Remember that before you even started looking for a new job, you had thoroughly evaluated your reasons for leaving your current employer and were truly ready to move on. Therefore, the possibility of accepting a counteroffer is out of the question.

A counteroffer is very counterproductive for all parties. First, it always distresses your current organization to discover that you would be willing to leave. Second, it communicates that your loyalty can be bought, so that even if the organization gave you more money or a different title to persuade you to stay, your managers would never trust you again. Third, you have little to gain from working for an organization that would not reward you with more money or a new title until you threatened to resign.

It is important to talk with people that you have enjoyed working with and thank them for their contributions. It is also advisable to keep in touch with key people after you leave. You need to maintain positive references for the future.

When discussing your resignation, never express negative thoughts or feelings about your current employer. Instead, focus on the growth and opportunity that the new position will offer.

You should have accepted your new position for all of the right reasons.

CHAPTER 15

The Three-Month Checkup

No matter how thorough your interview process was, by your third month at your new job, the honeymoon is usually over. After those first three months, we recommend that you take a moment to step back and assess the situation. Ask yourself:

- How am I doing in my new position?
- What is expected of me?
- What kind of feedback am I getting on the work I've completed?
- Am I being mentored / coached / trained?
- Will the new challenges that I face help me grow in my career?
- Did I make the right decision?
- Is my family happy?

Be sure to take a realistic approach. It has only been three months, and although you may have accomplished something, you obviously have not had the necessary time to achieve significant results. Even still, are you playing a vital role? Is your voice being heard? Are you doing what you were hired to do? Do you sense that opportunities for promotion will be available down the road?

Don't be afraid to ask your superior how you're progressing, what more you may need to learn, and so on. And consider the possibility that your peers can give you some hints as well.

It is imperative that you be totally committed to your new job, because when you encounter difficulties early on, you need to be able to shrug them off and keep going. It's easy to second-guess your decisions if you are not totally committed in the first place.

Make sure that you closely monitor your performance and regularly check in with your boss to make sure you are meeting his or her expectations. It is critical to keep abreast of the changing winds within your organization, and frequent updates with your boss and teammates will ensure that your goals and targets remain valid.

The best advice we can offer you for getting the most out of your new position is to be actively engaged. Volunteer to take on projects that will give you additional responsibility, increase your exposure to the organization and its people and offer new learning experiences. Think of creative ways to add value to your department or organization.

The first three months are sometimes shaky in terms of the adjustments you and your boss must make to work together effectively. Keep checking in to make sure you are on target. If you have negotiated a high salary, you will be watched carefully to see if you are adding value. Do your best to live up to expectations.

Your desire to do a good job may mean that you can't spend as much time with your family as you'd like, as you all adapt to your new lives. Keep the avenues of communication open and recognize that it will take time to restore the balance that you previously enjoyed. If you are single, you too must evaluate your comfort level with your new community and your world outside of work. Developing a comfortable support system is critical for anyone who relocates to a new community.

To really understand a new job takes at least a year, so be patient. If things aren't quite what you expected, don't be tempted to give up after only a few months. If, however, you encounter serious problems, leave your new job in less than a year so you won't appear indecisive. We all make mistakes. It's easy to make career errors if you are leaving a long-tenured job.

CHAPTER 16

Career-Limiting Mistakes

Despite their best efforts and intentions, people do things that keep them from being totally successful and even get them fired. As we have talked with candidates and clients over the years, we've collected many sad stories and seen a wide range of fatal flaws. Although a majority of career-limiting moves may seem trivial, they can be destructive and thus should be strictly avoided.

For example, job seekers are often tempted to misrepresent or embellish things about their education and accomplishments, particularly on a resume. Most organizations consider listing degrees that were never earned (even if the person went to college for four years) or misrepresenting previous work experience, dates of employment and the like as grounds for termination or withdrawal of an offer.

Many organizations will ask for copies of W2 forms before making an offer to ensure that a candidate has not exaggerated previous compensation. Criminal background checks, drug screening and pre-employment physicals are frequently required.

Based on our conversations with candidates who have lost positions and with clients who have recently removed incumbents, we have developed a list of common on-the-job mistakes that can have strong negative consequences.

One of the biggest mistakes people make is not communicating well and frequently, even when it is bad news. Keeping management, peers and employees well informed in language they can understand is critical. Verbal and written communication is essential. Letting people know in advance when there is a potential problem or a deadline that will be missed is vital. Hoping that no one will notice or that the problem will be solved by some miracle is never a good idea.

In healthcare organizations, it is critical to communicate with executives, peers and staff, both within the IT department and in all user departments. Physicians are powerful players and need to be handled appropriately. Being responsive and clearly explaining and answering questions are very important to physicians. Physicians respond to data. Ignoring their requests without proper communication can be career limiting.

Consistently over-committing will cost you your credibility. Agreeing to initiatives that you know will fail due to lack of resources, funding or approval from key constituents is extremely dangerous. You walk a fine line between appearing negative and uncooperative and being unrealistic. Success demands the proper research and due diligence, not just a "yes" response because someone powerful demands it.

Bringing in projects that are consistently late, over budget or both will attract much negative attention. Many CIOs in healthcare organizations have lost their positions because of not managing the consultants' and vendors' implementing systems and allowing costs to dramatically exceed the planned budget. If projects are late for the lab, and then pharmacy and then human resources, the word will spread and your credibility will be questioned. We have all found ourselves in this situation at least once. Learn from your mistakes, make sure each plan is feasible, and deliver what you promise.

IT is a service industry. Forgetting that is a sure way to severely limit your career. Customer service means more than giving users what they need. It involves listening, responding, explaining and fixing problems on a timely basis. Returning phone calls and e-mails promptly is important, no matter who the source. Nothing can cause more fury than a user who is repeatedly ignored. If a system is down in the ICU, nurses are severely impacted and patient care could be compromised. If a physician consistently has difficulty accessing the system from home, his frustration may boil over with serious repercussions. Responsiveness is critical.

Physicians are very fact- and information-driven users. They expect honest, accurate answers and explanations on a timely basis. Any project that affects physicians must be handled extremely carefully at every stage. Taking their time costs them money. Anything that negatively affects patient care puts them at risk. Losing the trust and respect of the physician community is very damaging and career limiting in the healthcare IT industry.

Persuading key decision makers is critical for success. Getting their buy-in and support requires excellent due diligence and planning that is communicated in a persuasive, well-documented manner. Without this buy-in and support, most projects are doomed to fail or are not considered valuable.

The inability to hire and retain excellent staff has many negative implications. Whatever must be done, no matter how unorthodox, to recruit and keep an outstanding team is critical to any leader's success. Projects will fall short and users will be angry if the right team is not in place. People who fail to build effective teams will be perceived as ineffective managers and poor leaders. Utilizing consultants over long periods of time, rather than filling the roles with employees can be very risky. It sends a message that you can't hire the right people or you don't trust the internal team.

A person who is not a team player and runs an autocratic IT department, dictating what is needed and by whom, will never be tolerated long-term. Eventually, the controlling approach taken by this self-important "expert" who mystifies IT with techno-babble will backfire. Involving users in decisions and giving them the knowledge they need to participate in solid decision making are critical for continued success. Even the most top-down people can and must change their behavior to make themselves more effective.

Getting on the wrong side of a powerful vendor or consulting firm is not a good approach. Certain organizations or people may respond with vindictiveness. Negative comments, whether true or not, can be very dangerous because they plant damaging seeds. Even in very negative situations, always be professional and polite. Do what is necessary without creating hostility that could backfire down the road.

Among the many other career-limiting behaviors are projecting a negative attitude, screaming at or disciplining employees inappropriately, rarely coming out of your office, wearing inappropriate clothing, using inappropriate language, going behind your boss's back and treating managers or support staff rudely. Almost all career killers can be eliminated with thought and effort. Remember that honesty, integrity and good communication are the foundations of any successful career.

Sometimes you may get caught in a political situation over which you have no control. In that case, you need to extricate yourself quickly. Doing so can be easier said than done if you have a family to consider and job opportunities are limited in your area. Nonetheless, swift action must be taken if your professional reputation and future career are at stake.

If it appears after several months that you have taken the wrong job, have the wrong boss or are in the wrong corporate environment, it is clear that you need to leave. If a situation is not going to work out, you should try to leave gracefully.

Your immediate concern might be that people reviewing your resume may think you are a job hopper. In fact, if you leave before one year, it will not look bad on your resume. Recruiters understand that people occasionally make bad job choices. However, if you linger on, you begin to look indecisive or run the risk of being terminated, rather than planning the move yourself.

CHAPTER 17

New Positions, Challenges and Opportunities for Growth in the Twenty-first Century

The healthcare IT job market continues to be strong, with many new positions emerging every year. That is good news. Also good news is the upswing in the number of internal hires. This means either that some excellent coaching and mentoring has been going on or that hiring executives are more willing to take chances on employees who they respect and trust, in the hopes that they can teach them the skills needed to assume new positions. It is your responsibility to work hard and gain the trust of others. By doing so, your career road map will be much easier to implement.

Lifestyle, location, and ability to grow within an organization are the strongest drivers for candidates that are seeking new positions. Following Y2K, the healthcare industry experienced tremendous change. All of that change created and continues to create opportunities for IT executives, managers and project leaders.

Because many of our leadership teams have paid attention to succession planning, now more than ever, we are seeing organizations promote from within. This is a great opportunity at all levels.

Here we are well into the twenty-first century. The nation's economic climate has been inconsistent. Although the healthcare industry is strong, it is not immune to economic recession. Does this present a picture of gloom and doom? No, it represents a picture of opportunity for IT professionals who wish to grow into new areas. Many organizations are reeling from being spun off after less-than-successful mergers. Senior management teams are turning over, outsourcers are knocking on every door and boards are getting more involved in operations.

This is a perfect time for you to reevaluate your resume and your career plan and become a valued and necessary employee who can assist your organization through this economic slump and all the related pressures, from both the government and business community. Be realistic about the positions you would like to consider. Build a resume and qualifications that will equip you to reach your goals. Keep management up-to-date on your accomplishments, goals, abilities and interest in supporting the organization. Pay close attention to the political winds and the potential changes in organizational direction. Be prepared to fill the empty spots. Be a team player and a producer. Go to every conference that your organization can afford, read every journal in your library and understand what the significant industry issues are going to be.

Try to forecast and create a role for yourself that will support your organization through a revamping of your current job or the creation of a brand new job. Try to stop worrying about the lack of money in your organization and begin to think about creatively utilizing your resources. Make sure that your leadership knows what you are doing. Keep leadership apprised of all your projects and ask for new growth opportunities as they arise.

Because some of the new positions are groundbreaking, few people have the experience necessary to fill them. It will follow that if you are the first person in your organization to obtain some of the skills and still retain some of your project management and deliverable schedules, you may be tapped for some great growth possibilities. This is not an opportunity to grab huge raises but rather an opportunity to be a team player. Do the best you can for your organization, and you will get noticed.

NEW POSITIONS

There is currently more activity in the healthcare IT job market than we have seen in several years. A lot of people left the provider side of healthcare to join e-health companies and other entrepreneurial organizations. Many of them have come back to the provider side or are involved in other related businesses. Many consulting firms have experienced a down turn since the boom years in the late '90s and 2000. Many of these individuals are also interested in returning to the provider side.

The Balanced Budget Act, HIPAA and huge clinical systems initiatives that include complete clinical transformation have forced healthcare organizations to look at new positions and expenses. Web-based technology and e-commerce solutions are also creating excitement and new opportunities. There is clearly a need to learn new things and contribute on a much broader scale.

HIPAA. HIPAA has created the need for
- Technical security positions
- Corporate HIPAA security officers
- Privacy officers

The demands of HIPAA are much broader and more complex than the challenges of Y2K. Most healthcare organizations are still not sure how to handle HIPAA. Everyone knows that it relates to security issues, and most organizations say they plan to add a security officer and / or related positions, but how many actually have? The wait-and-see attitude seems to be giving way to action as final HIPAA deadlines approach. The predictions of the past two years suddenly seem to be coming true, and exciting new roles in security are developing. This is an outstanding opportunity for health systems to bring in non-healthcare IT talent and develop those people into future leaders.

Is a security officer a technical or policy position? Or is it both?

There is a definite need for technical experts to deal with security issues. Such individuals will be dealing with things like firewalls, encryption, security guidelines and safe practices. They will make sure that the systems keep information secure—which is probably the easiest part of HIPAA. Extensive security talent exists in other industries such as banking, finance and the military.

There is also a need for corporate security and privacy officers. People in these positions report at a very senior level, make recommendations on policy and standards and must really understand issues such as patient privacy, data implications and current and emerging technologies. In large health systems, the corporate security officer may assume more of a consulting role for the individual hospitals and health systems. In organizations of all sizes, the person in this position will need to work very closely with the technical security people.

The Internet / Intranet Challenge. The Web is one of the most dramatic and exciting challenges (and opportunities) facing healthcare organizations today. What strategies to implement, who to reach and how, what technical approaches to take and which vendors to partner with are huge questions.

More and more healthcare organizations are recognizing that the Internet and intranets can improve the cost-effectiveness of internal systems, redesign care and actually affect patient populations.

The position of Internet strategist is rapidly becoming more common. Although this position is not really technical, its holder must work closely with the technology specialists and must "talk the talk." There is a clear need to understand healthcare. Frequently, the position reports to the vice president of marketing or strategic planning, not to IT.

Positions in consumer e-health applications focus on creating applications that are valuable and easy to use. The responsibilities are not unlike those in clinical or financial applications. The focus is on adding value by delivering more interactive, mutually beneficial applications, along with service and information, to consumers. People in these positions need solid understanding of both healthcare and systems.

The need for Web masters / developers has been growing. These individuals develop Web sites. They are not necessarily from healthcare (although such a background is a plus) and work daily with the more strategic players focused on the Web. The most successful Web endeavors are those that marry technology with creativity.

Other New Positions. Among the other new positions we are increasingly seeing are:

- Chief medical information officer (CMIO) / medical director of information technology
- Vice president of clinical transformation
- Clinical and EMR specialists / director of clinical systems
- Associate / deputy CIO
- Director, project management office
- Director, physician office information systems
- Director, healthcare IT finance

The hiring of CMIOs or medical directors of clinical systems is a growing trend. More physicians today than ever before are dedicating the majority of their time to IT.

Extensive clinical systems implementations, including CPOE, have caused many organizations to actively recruit for this role. Vendors and consulting firms have been aggressively hiring physicians who are IT savvy for key roles related to development, sales and delivery.

Most organizations that are doing systemwide implementations of clinical systems take advantage of the opportunity to completely re-design or transform how clinical care is delivered—as part of the new systems-installation process. As a result, vice presidents of clinical transformation are being hired by both health systems and consult-ing firms. Frequently, these roles are filled by IT-savvy physicians who take on a much broader role, combining the new systems initiatives with a total overhaul of how care is delivered to be more efficient, ef-fective and safe.

Other IT professionals with clinical backgrounds such as nursing, laboratory, pharmacy and radiology are in very high demand. They play roles from director / manager of clinical systems and project director of clinical systems initiatives to senior analysts, as well as take on implementation, development, sales and training roles for consult-ing firms and vendors. The implementation of robust clinical sys-tems, electronic patient records and integrated scheduling is under way. Superb project management skills and knowledge of structured methodologies are in demand.

The associate / deputy CIO, is increasingly valuable to today's CIO, particularly in complex organizations. More and more CIOs are being asked by senior management to add or identify this position. Depth is critical to survival in today's competitive environment. The associate / deputy CIO is not just an operations person, but is also the chief operating officer to the CIO, who is preparing to be the CIO.

With a very large number of established CIOs slated to retire within the next five years, we are at a critical point where successors must be groomed and developed to step up to CIO positions. If suc-cessors are not in place or if they have not been given the required mentoring, exposure and experience, health systems will fall into chaos. They will be faced with an enormous need and a limited pool of qualified candidates.

The director of the project management office is a new and excit-ing role that the CIO may have filled in the past. It requires skills in project management, business, administration and finance. Technical skills are not a critical factor. An MBA is a definite advantage.

The need for directors of physician office IT is growing. Most frequently this position reports to the CIO of the health system. The focus is on providing services and building liaisons with the physician groups. Sometimes this position is part of a for-profit company within the IT organization. The role generally involves marketing IT services to new physician groups. Quite often this director acts as an IT vendor and provides paid support to physician clients.

Nonacute care specialists are in high demand. As healthcare extends to the nonacute world, many organizations are retraining existing personnel or hiring new people to address all areas within the continuum of care. Ambulatory care, long-term care, home care and the like all require connectivity and specialized applications. As healthcare changes, technology advances and people live longer, more healthcare services outside the acute care setting will be required. The opportunities are tremendous.

Directors of healthcare IT finance are fairly new in our industry. We are seeing larger organizations that must deal with huge budgets and contracts hiring this role as a full-time position. As a result, increasing numbers of former CFOs or directors of finance are being hired to take leadership roles in developing procedures, monitoring budgets, avoiding cost overruns and ensuring that all IT initiatives are managed in a fiscally responsible manner.

IS THIS THE TIME TO BE AN ENTREPRENEUR?

Tremendous changes are taking place throughout the healthcare industry. With change comes opportunity, and entrepreneurs thrive on opportunity. So is this the time to make the leap?

Many of us have dreamed of running our own business, not being tied to the politics and schedules of a corporate position, and never again having to answer to a boss we don't respect. However, before you run out to start your own business, there are several issues that you need to consider carefully—even when this kind of work environment seems right.

Many entrepreneurs are viewed as mavericks. Being a maverick, a person who bucks the system and can't or won't hold on to a regular job, is no substitute for being a true entrepreneur. An entrepreneur is a creative risk-taker who has an idea for a business that is needed or will be needed based on current trends, outside forces and initiatives.

Before you quit your full-time job or if you've been laid off or fired, seriously consider your motivation for striking off on your own. Even if you have a burning desire to run your own business and have thoroughly researched an idea that you believe will fly, you must very carefully assess your tolerance for risk and your current financial picture. Although loans and other funding options may be available, you must determine how long you can go without a regular income stream.

If you're convinced you have what it takes, good luck! This could be the perfect time for you, because the healthcare industry is wide open and so many very specific opportunities lie ahead.

Given that some consulting firms have lost clients' trust due to their interest in staffing with very junior personnel or escalating fees, the door is wide open for independent consultants and small companies that have strong credibility and outstanding experience.

Specific, highly specialized skills are in extreme demand. Experts in fields such as security, HIPAA, and clinical systems implementation can write their own tickets, choosing from the many opportunities that existing firms do not cover well. Tremendous opportunities also exist for professionals who can coach and mentor both CIOs and CEOs on IT-related issues. To succeed in any of these initiatives, however, you must be a recognized expert who does an outstanding job. Repeat business, referrals and excellent references will be ensured.

Joining a small entrepreneurial firm is another way to become an entrepreneur without bearing all the risk yourself. Before joining such a firm, make sure you believe in the product or service, like and trust the leadership and are comfortable with the firm's financial position.

Tremendous opportunities exist today in the field of healthcare IT. New challenges are creating new positions. And as new technologies are developed, new accomplishments become possible. Starting over can be a good thing, especially when the circumstances are right. In such an environment, being creative and staying flexible are more important than ever before.

CHAPTER 18

Career Happiness

Given the mission and core values inherent in the healthcare field, a career in healthcare IT can be rewarding and satisfying. But to find true happiness and job satisfaction, you must listen to yourself and follow your passion. You will be happier and everyone around you will prosper as a result. The worst thing in life is doing something you don't like or don't find fulfilling. Of course, we all need to make a living, but we also need personal satisfaction.

KEY FACTORS FOR JOB SATISFACTION

We deal with people's career happiness and job satisfaction on a daily basis. Through our daily telephone interviews with candidates and our annual job satisfaction surveys, including the 2002 job satisfaction survey we conducted with HIMSS, we gather a great deal of in-depth information. As illustrated in Figure 18-1, 55 percent of the respondents to the HIMSS / Hersher 2002 Job Satisfaction Survey reported that they were either satisfied or extremely satisfied in their current position. Only 13 percent said that they were not satisfied.

Salary alone is not the key to happiness and career satisfaction. Salary needs to be appropriate for the position and in line with salaries at other comparable organizations, but a big salary will not compensate for job unhappiness. Many other factors contribute to the happiness and satisfaction that healthcare IT professionals report feeling. When asked what factors caused them to leave their last position, respondents to the HIMSS / Hersher survey ranked salary third, well after growth / challenge and lack of opportunity for advancement.

Many intangible factors lead to happiness on the job. Among the factors we hear repeatedly are the need for challenges and opportunities and the desire for more responsibility. Feeling empowered to make suggestions and changes in the work environment also influence satisfaction, as do autonomy, authority to make decisions, involvement in planning and support from your supervisor and the company's management team. Belief in the mission and values of the organization is critical to many healthcare IT professionals and is frequently what attracted them to the healthcare field in the first place.

BALANCING WORK AND LIFE

In the long run, career happiness can only be achieved if you manage to keep time for yourself and life outside of work. Balance is very important. Being successful requires the ability to set priorities and delegate appropriately. A "can-do" attitude does not mean that you must do everything yourself. Perfectionism is not a good trait if it means you are the only one capable of meeting your standards for a job or project. Great leaders know what projects to delegate and what projects require their personal strengths. Working in an environment that encourages and supports a healthy balance between work and life is very important for long-term career satisfaction and happiness.

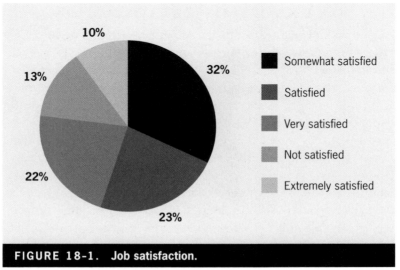

FIGURE 18-1.   Job satisfaction.

Source: HIMSS/Hersher 2002 Job Satisfaction Survey.

MONEY AND HAPPINESS

Even though salary may not necessarily be your primary motivator, it will still significantly contribute to your career happiness, so it merits discussion.

What is a "fair" salary?

Most of us want to feel that what we are being paid is fair both in terms of our position and the industry we work in. Many healthcare IT professionals do not know their market value until they decide to leave their current job or get a call from a headhunter or recruiter. Keep your ears open and educate yourself on the salary levels in your profession and in your region of the country. Look at industrywide salary surveys or seek out information at the public library, on the Internet or in trade publications. *Computerworld* annually conducts a comprehensive survey of salaries in various IT professions and industries, including healthcare, which can give you a basis for comparison.

As shown in Figure 18-2, 40 percent of the respondents to the HIMSS / Hersher 2002 Job Survey felt that they were not competitively paid, and 9 percent said that they didn't know.

Listen to recruiters when they call; they can greatly help you determine your market value. Establishing a relationship with a recruiter can keep you in touch with the market and give you fairly accurate salary ranges for jobs based on your skills and level of experience. If you are truly unhappy with your compensation, assemble

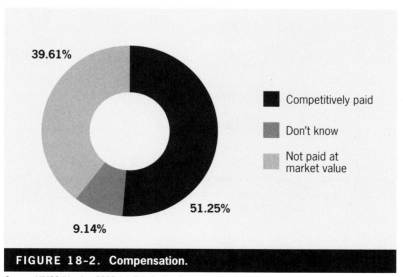

FIGURE 18-2. **Compensation.**

Source: *HIMSS/Hersher 2002 Job Satisfaction Survey.*

your facts and have an open discussion with your boss to see if there is a solution, such as taking on additional responsibilities.

Benefits and perks seem to enhance job satisfaction, but workers do not view them as critical. Leading the list of key benefits are performance-based bonus programs and tuition reimbursement. Basic benefits such as health insurance are considered a given. IT professionals value ongoing educational training, professional development, conference attendance and trade association membership. Paid time off and vacation time, followed by better retirement packages and health benefits, are also frequently cited as important to overall satisfaction. The areas in most need of improvement, as identified by the respondents to the 2002 HIMSS / Hersher survey, are displayed in Figure 18-3.

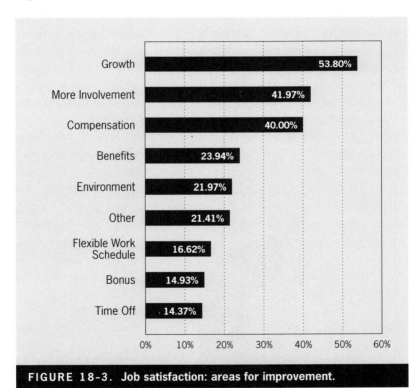

FIGURE 18-3. Job satisfaction: areas for improvement.

Source: HIMSS/Hersher 2002 Job Satisfaction Survey.

ASPIRATIONS

We all have our own unique motivations. Ask yourself what you want in your ideal job. What factors have contributed to your happiness in your previous positions? What factors have interfered with your happiness or satisfaction?

Develop a clear picture of the basics that you need to feel happy and satisfied. The factors that enticed people to leave their current positions as reported in the 2002 HIMSS / Hersher survey are identified in Figure 18-4, and the factors that persuaded people to accept new positions are presented in Figure 18-5.

When you consider new opportunities, be sure to evaluate the intangibles as carefully as you evaluate the tangibles. Self-worth, respect, flexibility, opportunities for growth and challenges are critically important to most of us. Don't overlook those factors, even if the salary is substantial.

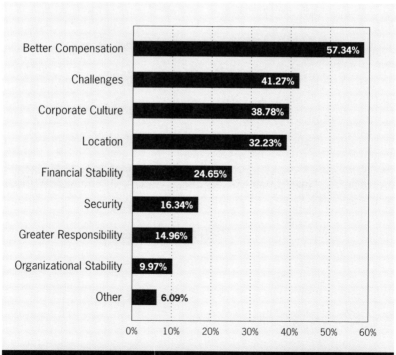

FIGURE 18-4. Enticements to leave current job.

Source: HIMSS/Hersher 2002 Job Satisfaction Survey.

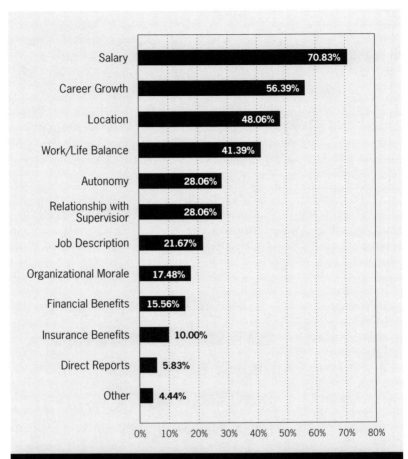

FIGURE 18-5. Factors for accepting a new job.

Source: HIMSS/Hersher 2002 Job Satisfaction Survey.

Conclusion

What will the next five years bring?

Delivery of healthcare is improving. We are looking closely at clinical outcomes. If we're lucky, many of us will be living much longer. And we will be living a little bit healthier. IT will be utilized heavily in this quickly changing environment.

So, how do these statistics affect the IT community?

These will be extremely exciting times. It will be increasingly important for people to be computer literate. We will all be paying our bills online, planning vacations online, shopping online and so on. In fact, many people are already doing most of these activities online.

We believe that more stakeholders in the healthcare industry—providers in particular—will soon realize the benefits of accurately knowing their patients' histories, no matter where those patients may have gone for healthcare in the past. Patients will feel much more secure knowing that all of their physicians have easy access to their full medical records. Because many people are expected to live longer, they are likely to develop illnesses that are chronic, and their medical histories need to be available to avoid crises.

Particularly, if we could work more with underserved populations, we could catch problems earlier and, as a result, significantly lower costs and increase quality of health. No matter how long we live, we will still be saddled with the fact that the majority of our healthcare costs will occur within the last five years of our lives. However, using information resources appropriately will keep consumers, physicians and payers more informed.

Clearly, security and privacy are key issues. However, we would prefer to have them as issues rather than excuses. Security and privacy have been among our excuses for not developing an electronic health record (EHR) for years.

As IT professionals, we need to build our careers as broadly as possible so that we will be prepared for new roles such as when more and more patients are treated at home. This will include seniors as well as young children.

Think of the advantages of catching an asthma attack early because a mother can e-mail or call during the middle of the night to share her concerns: "Someone tell me what to do!" And think of her relief when she actually receives clear, helpful instructions instead of having to wait until the doctor's office opens at nine o'clock in the morning or until someone calls back much later, perhaps after the situation has escalated and the family has been forced to visit an emergency room.

Of course, liability is a critical issue. We believe that liability concerns, as well as privacy and security, will be tackled very quickly. We have extremely informed consumers and a business community that is demanding accountability.

Now is the time to prepare yourself in whatever areas you feel need improving to be at the forefront of the information resources supporting the ever-evolving healthcare field. Healthcare policy may well be affected by the ability of everyone in the industry to communicate in an electronic mode.

It is the broad-based thinkers who will succeed. It is the creative CEO of the healthcare enterprise who will insist on connectivity to homes, physician offices, referring physicians and payers.

We will cut down on duplicate testing. Results will be easily accessible online. Physicians may even go so far as to automate and send us notices when patients are due for their annual exams. Car service organizations do it, as do drug stores. If they can do it, why can't our massive healthcare system figure it out? They will. And sooner than expected.

This will be an incredibly wild ride that will change on a daily basis. Rising insurance costs will unfortunately continue. We can hope that with a healthy, informed, aging population and with a very realistic look at the cost of procedures and medications, healthcare in general, as well as healthcare policy, will evolve and improve rapidly.

Automation will be there every step of the way and should contribute significantly to quality care.

What we perceived as very forward thinking, at year five is old hat, and by year six, we're ready to move on to new areas. Keep yourself up-to-date and ahead of the game. Pay attention to business trends and healthcare responses across the country. This is a very volatile time in our industry. Long-term CIOs are being fired. More and more clinical IT professionals are taking on key roles, and many organizations are looking for significant change.

As an industry, our product and our outcomes are the patients. IT has become the key driver of successful patient care and delivery.

Are you ready?

Index

H

Health Insurance Portability and Accountability Act of 1996 (HIPAA), 5, 9, 107

Healthcare Information and Management Systems Society (HIMSS), 36

HIMSS/Hersher 2002 Job Satisfaction Survey
    coach/mentor skills, 40f
    compensation, 115f
    most desirable skills, 30f
    job satisfaction, 114f
        areas for improvement, 116f

reasons for leaving last position, 68f
    enticements, 117f
    new job acceptance factors, 118f
    supervisor evaluations, 39f

I

Internal promotions, 49-57
    interview process, 50-52
    loyalty/commitment, 54-55
    succession planning, 53-54
    wrong reasons for, 55-57

Interview process, 65, 77-81
    and assessing corporate culture, 85-86
    follow-up interviews, 80-81
    and internal promotion, 50-52
    interviewing questions, 79-80
    needed outcomes, 79
    personal appearance, 78
    preparation for, 78

J

Job search, 67-76
    ads, 71
    and flexibility, 73-75
    networking, 71-73
        in academic healthcare environment, 73
    reasons for leaving last position, 68f
    recruiting firms, 70-71
    and rejection, 75-76